Preparing children for permanence

A guide to undertaking direct work for social workers, foster carers and adoptive parents

Mary Romaine with
Tricia Turley and Non Tuckey

BAAF
ADOPTION
& FOSTERING

Published by
British Association for Adoption & Fostering
(BAAF)
Saffron House
6–10 Kirby Street
London EC1N 8TS
www.baaf.org.uk

Charity registration 275689

© BAAF, 2007

British Library Cataloguing in Publication Data
A catalogue record for this book is available from the British Library

ISBN 978 1 905664 07 8

Edited by Hedi Argent
Project management by Shaila Shah
Illustration on cover by Victoria A McGuire
Designed by Andrew Haig & Associates
Typeset by Fravashi Aga, London
Printed in Great Britain by the Lavenham Press
Trade distribution by Turnaround Publisher Services, Unit 3, Olympia Trading
Estate, Coburg Road, London N22 6TZ

BAAF is the leading UK-wide membership organisation for all those concerned
with adoption, fostering and child care issues.

Contents

1	Introduction	1
2	What is meant by permanence?	3
3	Legal forms of permanence	7
4	What is direct work?	10
5	Establishing a relationship with the child	16
6	Preparing for the work	20
7	Planning and managing sessions	27
8	Child protection issues	34
9	Communicating with children	37
10	Giving children information and undertaking life journey work	45
11	Helping children develop positive identity and build resilience	56
12	Ascertaining children's wishes and feelings	67
13	Helping children think about a new permanent family	70
14	Staying in touch: talking with children about contact	75
15	Helping children with separations and losses	82
16	Working with sibling groups	87
17	Introductions and moves to a new family	94
18	Disengaging	101
19	Making sense of disruptions	105
20	References	108
21	Bibliography	110
22	Appendix 1: Communication tools and age groups	112
23	Appendix 2: Index of activities	113
24	Appendix 3: Suggested contents for workers' "tool kits"	114

Acknowledgements

The authors are indebted to the following persons and organisations for their invaluable help:

Foster carers Ahmet, Cheryl, Chris, Irene, Jamie and Pete for their stories and case examples.

Karen Williams for the story of Molly Bear and for her general advice and support.

The Project Advisory Group: Carol Floris, Dr Carolyn Sampeys, Freda Lewis, Mike Burns, Rachel Talbot and Rhonwyn Dobbing for their professional advice, direction and support.

Barbara Hutchinson, Deputy Chief Executive, BAAF, for her professional advice.

Hazel Jewkes and Val Leung for their administrative support (and sense of humour).

Hedi Argent for editing this edition.

The authors are particularly indebted to the Welsh Assembly Government for providing the financial support for writing and publishing this guide.

Note

This guide was initially written as part of a commission for the Welsh Assembly Government. It was distributed to all local authorities in Wales in 2005. This edition is a revised version and has been made relevant and applicable to all parts of the UK.

The authors

Mary Romaine joined BAAF in 1993 as a Consultant Trainer and was appointed as Director of BAAF Cymru in 1997. She has a background in community development within the voluntary sector, including the promotion of volunteering, rural communities support and social care for people affected by HIV/Aids.

Tricia Turley has extensive experience in the field of child placement, having worked with children being fostered and adopted since the 1970s, both in London and Wales. She was responsible for setting up a highly regarded fostering scheme for adolescents in South Wales early in the 1990s. Most recently, she coordinated an innovative consortium of adoption agencies in South Wales.

Non Tuckey has experience of managing a range of social work teams, including child protection and children and families teams. She was a Consultant Trainer with BAAF for three years, leaving to become an Area Director for CAFCASS Cymru.

Introduction

Do you know where you were born, at what time, your birth weight, when you first walked and talked, when you went to playgroup, each house you lived in and who in the family you look like? Many children who have been separated from their original families do not know such basic facts about their early lives. Some will have lost all sense of their own histories.

It must be disconcerting. It must provide an uncertain basis for growing up.

Children being placed with new permanent families are often contending with moves from poorly understood pasts to what may be very different but equally unknown futures. *Preparing children for permanence* describes the focused work that is needed to enable children and young people to make this difficult transition with some confidence.

Children for whom we are planning adoption or other permanent placements are likely to experience a range of intense, perhaps conflicting, emotions, and to have many voiced and unvoiced questions. Their early years and foster placements may have had a profound impact on how they regard family life. How safe is it? What does love and care mean in this family? How can I best survive here? What will happen to people in my first family? Will I ever see my grandmother again? What will these new people think of me and why are they doing this?

We know, from what children tell us, that preparation for permanence from empathetic, trusted adults can make a difference to how children approach and experience family transitions. Indeed, without planned and focused direct work with children, the risk factors for placement disruption can be high.

Direct work, including life journey work, is an essential and integral part of planning for permanence for children. It should be undertaken by someone the child knows and trusts. Ideally, for looked after children, this will be their social worker, with the support of their foster carer or other trusted adult. Local authorities can be said to be fulfilling their duties to children only if this work is resourced and supported appropriately. If, as a matter of necessity, the work has to be allocated to a worker who is new to the child, it is crucial to have time for the child and worker to get to know each other. In any event, direct work is not an optional extra in permanence planning – it is *fundamental*.

This guide is a resource for social workers and others who are planning, undertaking and evaluating direct work with looked after children for whom a permanent placement is being planned. It will assist foster carers if children are to stay with them permanently as well as those who will be helping children to move on. It will also be of help to adoptive parents who are welcoming sons and daughters into their family.

Although this guide is not intended for children and young people, it incorporates the principles that children's views should be taken into account when planning and providing services, and that children should be supported in participating in decisions about their futures.

When, for ease of reference, we refer to "children" in the text, this should be taken to mean both children and young people.

A variety of activities to use in direct work are described throughout this guide. They can be adapted for use with younger or older children. Many older children will still enjoy the opportunity to indulge in "younger child" activities. It is important to find the right level for children whose developmental age differs from their chronological age.

The focus throughout this guide is on practice development in direct work with children. It therefore does not cover:

- assessment;
- court work;
- children's statutory reviews;
- adoption support planning;
- working with the panel;
- working with birth families;
- inter-agency work.

The guide sets out responsibilities for both social workers and foster carers and, in relevant sections, guidance for adoptive parents. It is based on the principle of working together in partnership to achieve effective outcomes for children in permanent placements.

What is meant by permanence?

Being and belonging

Most children never have to question who their family is. They may at times feel like distancing themselves, but they do not stop being part of their family. They therefore grow up with a deep-rooted sense of belonging to a connected set of people whom they can always claim and who have a claim on them. Even when we are adults, family members can provide a "backstop" when we are let down by others. This fundamental sense of belonging also contributes to the development of a positive identity – a clear idea of who we are and how we fit into the world.

In contrast, children who have been effectively separated from their birth families and who may have experienced a number of placements are likely to have had their sense of belonging and personal identity challenged, and probably fragmented. Their overall experience can lead them to expect that all families are temporary and conditional – people with whom you live for a while subject to certain conditions. Children and young people with these experiences may become skilled in managing relationships which lack continuity and are often superficial.

Some children will, over time, come to feel more comfortable with such relationships – they understand them, and feel they have less danger of being hurt. If children have moved many times, they may have had little opportunity to learn about emotionally close and enduring relationships. They may profoundly mistrust their own ability to love or to be loved and included in a nurturing family. Some children will regard any "down" in the normal "ups and downs" of family life as signalling an end to the placement. Sometimes children will disrupt placements themselves rather than wait for what, in their view, is inevitable.

Foundations for family life

Developing the personal foundations that help children comprehend and feel confident in "for better, for worse" relationships takes time if they have had an unstable history. These personal foundations include a cognitive understanding about what it means to be permanently in a family and an emotional competence that allows enduring reciprocal affection and empathy.

Prior to a permanent placement, many children will learn from foster carers who purposefully model positive aspects of family relationships and who encourage children to develop pro-social (as opposed to anti-social) coping skills. Most importantly, foster carers can support social workers in helping children to own their histories and to have a more hopeful view of their futures.

In summary, permanence enables children:

- to develop a sense of belonging;
- to have a sense of security;
- to know their future is certain;
- to develop close, trusted familial relationships;
- to acquire a "secure base" in attachment terms;
- to develop a robust, positive identity.

Permanent family options for children and young people include:

- returning home to their birth family;
- living with a relative or other person close to them, by virtue of a residence order or a special guardianship order or no order;
- living long term with foster carers, who may or may not be related, and remaining within the looked after system;
- being adopted.

"Permanence" implies that the family relationships forged in childhood and adolescence will continue beyond independence. When an adult, he or she will continue to be a member of this family, and any of their children will also belong to the family. The first and last options listed above have this as an intended outcome, but of course there are no guarantees. The other two options may result in a family for life, but the legal framework does not secure it, and the usual expectation is that the child will leave the home at 16 or 18 years.

The essential factor for children is that they are able to make affirming, enduring relationships in whichever is the appropriate placement for them – this means that support for children and families must be made available beyond any court order. Preparation for permanence is simply the first part of continuing support for permanence.

Permanence and family transition

It is difficult for us, as adults, to comprehend the enormity of change for children who will not return to their birth families. Much that a child has taken for granted about his or her identity and place in the world is taken away.

Imagine this:

- **I will never live with my mother again, or my father.**
- **I may never see my brother/sister.**
- **My name is different.**
- **My school is different.**
- **I have lost all the friends I used to have.**

- **I have to leave my foster mum.**
- **I am four years old.**

Children have little control over the process of being accommodated and separated from their birth families. Social workers need to acknowledge this imbalance of power and the intense feelings that may result. Direct work can help children to feel valued and that their views and opinions matter.

Growing up with foster carers

Children growing up in long-term foster care can ease gradually into the relationship and into the wider family life. Studies show that outcomes, on the whole, are very good. But short-term placements are too often extended into long-term ones only because an original plan for a child to return to their birth family has drifted on too long. No matter how positive a placement is, it cannot be helpful for a child to have to live with an uncertain future for a protracted period.

As soon as it becomes clear that a child's welfare needs will not be met by a return home, an alternative plan for permanence, which may be to remain in the current foster placement, should be made without further delay. Even where children have already developed relationships with foster carers and their extended family, if the placement becomes permanent, many children will still need much support in relation to their not returning home, and much reassurance about not moving again.

Growing up with relatives

Growing up with relatives can be the most suitable placement option for many children. It means that they stay connected to their birth families and that issues of identity and belonging are made easier for them.

In terms of preparation for permanence, it should be recognised that, although children know and may love the relative or other person who will be raising them, they may still feel very sad or anxious about being separated from one or both birth parents or from siblings. Children can also be understandably uncertain about who has parental responsibilities for them, and about divided loyalties and conflicts in the family.

Being adopted

Adoption can represent the most radical change for children. However, the outcomes for adopted children are generally very positive, especially where the child has been well prepared for the move, and the family is provided with access to adoption support services.

Children being adopted will be permanently separated from everyone in their original family (except siblings, in cases where they are being adopted together); they will no longer have any legal connection with them, even if they continue to have some contact.

Social work practice has evolved to help adopted children experience the transition as part of a continuum, so that the legal cut-off does not give children a sense of being separated from their own histories. Preparation for permanence for children being placed for adoption should be seen as the beginning of ongoing support for children as they grow into adulthood.

Adoption support which is tailored to the specific needs of each child should be assessed and made available from the time of the original permanence plan. Local authority adoption agencies have duties to provide counselling and assistance to adopted children, after placement and after adoption – this is a legal requirement in England, Wales and Scotland.

Workers' and carers' perspectives on permanence options for children

Adults' views about what constitutes beneficial family life for children can be deeply embedded in our personal histories and professional lives. Permanence planning can challenge our views about what is best for children.

One question that frequently provokes debate is whether to move a child from a foster carer, with whom he or she has lived since infancy, to new adoptive parents. Of course, the decisions will vary depending on the needs of the individual child, but the adults involved may well apply different benchmarks or paradigms depending on their own personal and professional experiences.

exercise

Think about the respective benefits and drawbacks of the range of permanence options described above.

Can you associate any personal or professional experiences and values with your considerations about them?

What points would you make in discussions about whether to move a child from a foster carer, with whom he or she has a secure attachment, to new adoptive parents?

Legal forms of permanence

Foster care

The majority of looked after children in the UK are placed in foster care. Foster carers are registered and supported by a local authority or independent agency.

Foster carers do not, by virtue of being carers, acquire parental responsibility for the child. Parental responsibility remains with the birth parents and is shared with the local authority if a care order is in force. Even if a child grows up in their foster family, the legal relationship with them will not change.

If foster carers wish to acquire parental responsibility for a child being looked after, they have to apply for a residence order, a special guardianship order or an adoption order.

Residence orders

A residence order can be made in favour of a person who is related to a child or is otherwise close to a child, so that the child has a legal basis for living with that person.

A residence order is an order which settles the arrangements to be made as to the person with whom a child is to live. (Although residence orders exist in all parts of the UK, there may be subtle differences in the extent of parental responsibility held or not held by the person with the residence order.

The application cannot be made by a local authority.

A residence order discharges any existing care order; in consequence, the child is no longer looked after by the local authority and the local authority does not retain any parental responsibility, although a residence support allowance may be payable. The scale of this allowance varies but may be enhanced to meet special needs. A residence order can remain in force until a child reaches 16 years. If the person making the application is not the parent or guardian of the child, the court can direct that the order stands until the child is 18.

In considering an application for any order, the court must treat the welfare of the child as paramount and must take into account the child's ascertainable wishes and feelings; the child's physical, emotional and educational needs; any likely change of circumstances; all the child's relevant characteristics; any risk of harm to the child; and the capability of each parent and any other relevant person. The court is required to consider its whole range of powers and to be satisfied that making an order is better for the child than not doing so. The court can order a report from a Welsh Family Proceedings Officer, a Children's Guardian in England, a Curator *ad litem* in Scotland and a guardian *ad litem* in Northern Ireland.

Special guardianship

A special guardianship order has been introduced in England and Wales to provide greater stability for the child than a residence order.

Some children who are not able to return home but for whom adoption is not appropriate, may be living with, or could live with, a person who could assume parental responsibility for them, including current foster carers. A special guardian is entitled to exercise parental responsibility for the child (with certain exceptions) to the exclusion of any other person with parental responsibility. An allowance is payable depending on circumstances.

The Children Act 1989, as amended by the Adoption and Children Act 2002, provides that an application for a special guardianship order can be made by:

- any guardian of the child;

- a person in whose favour a residence order is in force in respect of the child or anyone who has the consent of all those in whose favour a residence order is in force;

- anyone with whom the child has lived for at least three years out of the last five years;

- where a care order is in force, anyone with the local authority's consent;

- in any other case, anyone who has the consent of all those with parental responsibility for the child;

- a local authority foster carer* with whom the child has lived for a period of at least one year immediately preceding the application;

- anyone else, including the child, who has leave of the court.

In considering an application for a special guardianship order, the court must treat the welfare of the child as paramount and consider the suitability of the applicant alongside all relevant matters. The court must also consider whether a contact order should be made and whether any other standing order should be varied or discharged.

Adoption

A child becomes adopted by virtue of the making of an adoption order. An adoption order removes parental responsibility completely and permanently from the child's birth parents and, where held, from the local authority and gives parental responsibility wholly to the adoptive parents. An adoption allowance, which is usually means tested, may be paid to meet the child's needs.

Adopted children gain full legal status in their adoptive family and cease entirely to have any legal relationship with their previous family. Throughout the UK, if, for example, a birth parent wanted their child to inherit from them, they would have to make provision in their will following an adoption order.

* By virtue of the Children Act 1989 S23, this includes foster carers registered with independent agencies.

An adopted person is treated in law as if born as the child of the adopters or adopter.

An adoption order can be made either with the consent of those with parental responsibility or where their consent has been dispensed with by the court and, in either case, where a placement order is in force. For agency placements, a child must have lived with the prospective adopters for 10 weeks before an adoption application can be made.

In considering an application for an adoption order, the court must treat the welfare of the child throughout life as paramount, and must be satisfied that making an adoption order is better for the child than not making an order.

Although an adopted child no longer has any legal relationship with their previous family, he or she may continue to have contact with some previous family members either by letters or, less commonly, face to face. When an adopted young person is 18 years old, he or she has the right to access information about their registered birth and the circumstances of their adoption.

Legal requirements to undertake direct work

Article 12 of the United Nations Convention on the Rights of the Child (UNCRC), ratified by the UK Government in 1991, states that:

> *States Parties shall assure to the child who is capable of forming his or her own views the right to express those views freely in all matters affecting the child, the views of the child being given due weight in accordance with the age and maturity of the child.*
>
> *For this purpose, the child shall in particular be provided the opportunity to be heard in any judicial and administrative proceedings affecting the child, either directly, or through a representative or an appropriate body, in a manner consistent with the procedural rules of national law.*

Planning for looked after children – permanence plans

The care plan for a looked after child must include a permanence plan. The permanence plan may be based on a "twin-track" approach, incorporating both a primary and an alternative plan.

The permanence plan must:

- reflect the child's wishes and feelings according to age and understanding. These must be recorded and taken into account when drawing up the plan for permanence. Any reasons for not following the child's wishes must be explained to the child and also recorded;

- ensure proper preparation of the child for the transition to permanence, including life journey work;

- incorporate assessment and planning for support services;

- include arrangements for contact.

What is direct work?

Direct work offers a child or young person the opportunity to explore, with a trusted adult, aspects of their life history which relate in some way to proposals for the future. The issues that may be raised can be very sensitive and the times spent together can be intense.

All direct work, no matter what the objectives are in the individual case, should help children to understand what has happened to them in the past, to know why they are where they are at present, and to feel more confident about moving into the future. Many children who are separated from their birth family have fragmented memories. Direct work can enable them to put the pieces of their lives together again; it should make them feel valued as unique individuals, encourage them to express preferences and to have a say in plans for permanence. Young people, on the whole, do not experience assessments as empowering and this work should therefore aim to contribute to raising self-esteem and building relationships. Empowered children have greater personal resources. Empowered children feel they have more understanding of and influence over their own lives and so have less need to attempt to control everything and everyone around them.

Objectives of direct work

- To give children information about their backgrounds and family circumstances.

- To help children make sense of their life history and present situation.

- To offer children a safe and contained space to explore and express a range of emotions.

- To ascertain children's wishes and feelings.

- To help children develop a positive sense of self.

- To help children deal with family transitions.

Direct work has evolved as an effective means of helping children explore personal identity, feelings about families and hopes and dreams for the future. Children and young people often find it easier to deal with ideas and feelings in the context of shared activity rather than formal discussions. Direct work can therefore be described as "play with a purpose".

Part of direct work, which is a shared activity between adult and child, should include a mixture of "free play" or activity as well as more structured play or activities.

Free play/activity

This is a period where the child or young person can choose from a range of materials (described in Appendix 1 and following), and the adult will take their cue from the child about whether:

- simply to observe the child in individual play; or

- to respond, with what may be an intermittent or running commentary, by reflecting back the child's words so the child can develop a theme; or

- gently to encourage the activity by asking what is happening or what might happen given different circumstances; or

- to join more fully in the activity.

Workers can sometimes find that they want to guide the child during free play in a direction that they have planned, but this would move it away from being true "free play", which can in itself have many benefits.

- It allows a child or young person to settle into the session or into a more formal shared activity.

- It provides the child with opportunities to explore a new direction following on from a previous session.

- It gives the child permission to express emotions freely.

Ellie always made her teddy say what she was afraid to say, and she made her dolls be angry while she herself tried desperately to please.

Workers should let children lead the play but invite them to develop thoughts and themes. What is a particular picture the child has drawn or is looking at about? Or, who are these puppets supposed to be? Repeating back the child's words will encourage him or her to enlarge on a theme or story. Each individual child will play and engage differently with the materials. The worker should be flexible and ready to follow where the child leads.

Structured play/activity

A variety of games and activities are helpful for the various purposes of direct work. A number of these are described in the relevant sections of Chapters 10 and following.

Involving others

All direct work will be made significantly less effective if the key worker fails to collaborate with others who know the child. It is important to make a list of significant people and consult with them prior to beginning the work and as appropriate during the course of the work. The child or young person should be aware, as the work proceeds, with whom the worker has discussed the various issues and may want to talk through the implications of sharing information with other named people.

Concerns and dilemmas

Going fast/going slow

A major dilemma for the worker can be balancing children's needs for exploration and understanding – which have their own momentum – with the timetabled planning of family placement work and court proceedings. The two are inextricably connected. Local authorities and courts are rightly obliged to take into account children's wishes and feelings when making decisions, but they may have to make them before the child has been properly heard, or a permanent placement opportunity may arise either too early or too slowly to coincide with a child's "readiness" to join a new family.

The aim should be to develop direct work at a pace that is comfortable and effective for the individual child. This may be more slowly than anticipated or, in some cases, more quickly. The approach will vary depending on the developmental age of the child or young person, but direct work must never be allowed to become submerged by all the other demands of family placement work.

Conflicting messages

Twin-track planning can mean that conflicting messages are being given to children by different adults about what is most likely to happen. One aim will be to try to set out clearly what the most likely options are and who will be involved in making decisions. The best way forward will be to use some of the games and exercises set out in Chapter 11 to clarify the various options and processes of decision-making.

Getting somewhere

There is often an understandable desire on the part of the adult to see clear "progress". Workers with a child's well-being at heart may naturally wish to reach a point where the child is becoming less distressed or where the child can communicate his or her wishes and feelings. We all have hopes and fears for the children we work with and look after – we want them to heal, to laugh more, to have safe futures. Our caring about what happens to children contributes to our being good social workers or good foster carers.

We must remember, however, that children who have lived through protracted periods of uncertainty may be unable to embrace optimism for a long time. Children who have never been offered choices will struggle to identify a preference. Some children may be wary of any one-to-one attention from an adult. Children who have been neglected or abused can find it hard to be aware of how they feel physically, let alone emotionally.

Many children will have very low self-esteem, which will inhibit their involvement with direct work. Other children will have developed defensive strategies that can make them resistant to change. We must bear in mind that direct work is often a measured, gradual process. If we keep good records, we will more easily be able to track progress in our work with individual children.

Confidence

Sometimes workers may not be confident about giving children information that will be difficult for them to hear. They can be anxious about being able to help children who are experiencing extreme emotions. They may feel they do not know enough to be able to answer children's questions.

Children and young people are more likely to remember how you related to them – that you listened, that you always arrived on time, that you were honest in admitting when you didn't have an answer – than to feel let down because you used the "wrong" words or were hesitant.

It is important to identify which issues are likely to be the most unsettling for the individual child. What will be the options for addressing these with the child? Who else can support the child during this particular piece of work? What personal resources does the child have to draw on?

How is he or she likely to respond and what strategies can be put in place to deal with this?

Working in age-appropriate ways

Children aged between two and four years

From around two years old, children learn to hold images in mind. They will play alone or in parallel with others. They are still self-centred and not yet quite ready to share. They start to develop a clearer understanding of self and others. They begin to play "pretend" games. The vocabulary of an average two-year-old is around 300 words. Children of this age can "catch" fears from adults. They can experience fear at separation and "spatial" fears.

Play helps pre-school children to integrate "good" and "bad" aspects of self and to forgive themselves for making mistakes (imaginary friends can often play a part here). Direct work through play can help to develop the emerging self, extend engagement with the world and with others, and support the child in transition to feel safe.

Children aged around four to seven years

Children in this age group still have little capacity for abstract thinking. They tend towards "magical" thinking (wishes make things come true) and egocentric thinking (they are responsible for everything that happens to them and others feel the same way about things as they do).

Children from the age of four can understand the concept of practising to learn a new skill. Many of the skills learnt through play will involve interactions with others. Story-play can help us understand how children see their world, so that we can cue in to their ideas about the future. We need to explore and re-explore each child's perceptions – they will be different from those of other children and of the adults involved. Play can teach children how things are done (going to school, bedtime routines, moving house) and can help the child to examine different kinds of families and relationships. Building and improving relationships are key aims of working with children. Even at the lower end of this age group, guided play can clearly reveal children's anxieties and feelings about what is happening around them.

Typical six-year-olds are physically very active. They often aspire to more than they can easily accomplish, leading to frustration or to lots of "starting things" with fewer "completing things". They can revert to infantile behaviour in parallel with wanting to be treated as "big". They need praise and clear boundaries.

CASE EXAMPLE
ROBIN

Pete was working with Robin, aged four, to prepare him for a move from his foster carers, with whom he had lived since he was six months, to a new adoptive family. Much of the guided play that Pete undertook with Robin centred on the forthcoming move. One day when Pete and Robin were moving a play figure to a new home, Robin frowned at Pete and said, 'The bed will be sad.' 'What bed, Robin?' 'The little boy's bed.'

Children aged seven to ten years

Children make a considerable leap in cognitive abilities in these years, which has an effect on how they perceive current and past life events. They can gain new understanding of their early years' experiences which can, in turn, result in behaviour changes. For example, children who have been separated from their birth families can re-assess their loss and embark on a process of "adaptive grieving", provoking distress or anger (Brodzinsky and Schechter, 1993). Children demonstrate concrete thinking at this age and find it difficult to understand alternative points of view, but it is easier than with younger children to help them explore their own changing perceptions.

An added purpose of direct work in these years might be to assist children to disengage appropriately from birth parents and others. We can help them to better understand the past, to make more sense of the present and to begin to contribute towards planning for their future. We can help them, through play, to explore more complex feelings and memories. Play can significantly assist identity formation, and can help children to learn and apply social rules and boundaries.

Children and young people aged nine years and upwards

Children begin to develop inductive reasoning (inferring a general law from particular instances), and deductive reasoning (inferring from the general what will happen in the particular instance). With increased cognitive abilities they are able to think hypothetically and in the abstract, and to learn that there are two sides to every story. They can consider different approaches to problems and foresee consequences from different actions. In adolescence, early unmet needs can come back to haunt the young person in an exaggerated form; however, this can also offer an opportunity to re-address these unmet needs and to meet them more appropriately, leading to lifelong changes.

Young people are more able to articulate how they are feeling and to explore with a trusted adult how they might approach difficult issues. We can, through play and shared activity, help them to develop a stronger sense of self, and to deal with present hurts without acting out or re-living past hurts, and to start to take on some of the responsibilities of adulthood. We can help them to think ahead, and to prepare for times when the effects of past traumas are most likely to surface. Above all, we can encourage young people to make an informed investment in permanence.

Older children can grieve for the loss of what otherwise might have been. We can help them to develop and practise a "public" story about their childhood that they feel comfortable with – a shortened, not too revealing version of the truth.

Regressing

When children are faced with situations that they cannot comprehend and cannot cope with, their only recourse may be to regress to younger behaviour patterns and ways of relating to people. If this happens during direct work, the approach should be adapted accordingly.

CASE EXAMPLE
EMLYN

Emlyn was placed with Joe and Nick when he was six years old. He had had a number of placements which had disrupted because of his hyperactive behaviour. His new foster carers were successful in establishing effective boundaries for him but it was clear that Emlyn was operating at a much younger age than six.

One day in the supermarket Emlyn grabbed a baby's bottle from the shelf and demanded that Nick take it home. Emlyn was good at supermarket tantrums and, on this occasion, Nick decided that it would do no harm to give in.

Emlyn instituted "baby time" in the evening, when he would ask to be fed from the bottle and cuddled like a baby. Joe and Nick discussed this with their social worker and it was agreed to let Emlyn regress but to "wean" him. Baby time was limited to 10 minutes and after a month Emlyn was ready to substitute a sports drinking bottle, which he held himself while still being cuddled. A little while later Emlyn was happy to have "family time" when he would sit next to Nick on the sofa with his sports bottle of juice, having a story read to him.

Developmental delay

Children may understand the world in ways that are less developed than their chronological age would suggest – that is, children's operational age may differ from their chronological age.

There can be a number of reasons for this:

- the child has an inherited or acquired organic condition;

- the child has been abused and/or neglected;

- the child has been moved, perhaps more than once, between placements;

- the child has been restricted in having opportunities (or being able to use opportunities) to develop cognitive, motor or sensory skills.

In many cases a medical adviser will not be able to give a conclusive explanation for developmental delay or to make an assured prognosis for future development. Social workers, foster carers and adopters should relate to children at their developmental level, and not attempt to make children function at their chronological age.

Establishing a relationship with the child

Direct work involves developing a relationship with a child. The child should feel that workers and carers are empathetic and accessible.

Social workers

Getting started

In order to have a relationship you will, of course, need to get to know the child or young person. Social workers will already have read the files fully and carefully and talked with the child's foster carers and others who know or have known the child well. When you start direct work you may have been the child's social worker for some time or you may be introducing yourself to the child for the first time. In either case, you should make sure that the child or young person has a clear, age-appropriate understanding of your role. Many children, even those who are used to having social workers, have only a vague and often inaccurate idea of what social workers actually do. If asked, they may say:

- 'My social worker got me a computer for my bedroom.'

- 'Social workers turn up and take you to the cafe.'

- 'Well, they are always late.'

- 'They're scary because they took me away from my mum.'

exercise

Think about children or young people you have helped to prepare for permanence.

How did you help them understand your role when you first met them?

What, if anything, might you change? Why?

Ask others – your manager, colleagues, foster carers and young people – how they think children see you when you start to work with them.

CASE EXAMPLE
JOSH

Hazel had been Josh's social worker for two years and was the person who had taken him from his birth family when he was six and placed him with foster carers. When she began direct work with Josh, Hazel wrote on pieces of paper all her tasks and roles as his social worker. She read each one out to him as she laid them on the floor. Josh then chose the ones he thought were right and was invited to add any more. This enabled Josh to voice his feelings about Hazel and his relationship with her, in a way that was not too direct or confrontational.

exercise

Read through Mark's story below. If you were Mark's new social worker, following the disruption of his adoptive placement, how might you introduce yourself to him? How would you describe your role to him and talk about the work you are planning?

CASE EXAMPLE
MARK

Mark is six years old. He has a sister, Kelly, aged three-and-a-half. Mark and Kelly's parents are Donna and Sean. Donna has learning difficulties and Sean has mental health problems. When Mark was born he and Donna were placed in a mother and baby unit for an assessment of Donna's parenting skills. Sean visited regularly, apart from a three-month period when he was in hospital. Donna, Sean and Mark were given a flat two blocks away from Donna's mother when Mark was one. They received lots of support from her and Donna's aunt and from the local authority. Mark was slow in reaching his developmental milestones but when he started nursery he improved quickly. Kelly was born prematurely and needed to be ventilated for several weeks.

Sean became very depressed and was admitted to the psychiatric hospital again. Donna spent all her time at the hospital and Mark was cared for by Donna's mother and aunt. Kelly came home at three months of age and Mark's care was shared between Donna, her mother and her aunt. Mark became devoted to Kelly.

Kelly began having fits when she was one. Mark witnessed some of these and became very protective of Kelly, and scared of ambulance workers.

Sean's mental health was deteriorating and he remained in hospital. Donna's mother died suddenly when Mark was four-and-a-half. Donna became very depressed and she began to reject the children. Mark stopped attending school and seemed to be looking after Kelly.

The children were accommodated on an interim care order with short-term carers when Mark was four-and-three-quarters. The placement lasted only three weeks as the carers had three other children and were unable to cope with Kelly's medical needs.

The children moved to a second very experienced carer, Molly. Kelly's health continued to cause concern and she was hospitalised for tests when Mark was five. The results showed that Kelly had a congenital heart problem that was likely to be life threatening. It was decided that the children would need to be separated. Mark was to be placed for adoption and long-term specialist carers were to be found for Kelly. A family was identified for Mark when he was six.

Mark appeared to settle well with his new family. The adopters had a birth daughter three years older than Mark, and initially they seemed to get on well. Mark began to form a very strong bond with the adoptive father and at weekends followed him constantly. This caused the daughter to feel very jealous. In addition, Mark talked all the time about missing his sister, which made her feel unwanted.

The adopters reported that their daughter was becoming unruly in school and spiteful toward Mark. They felt the placement was putting their daughter's wellbeing at risk. After six months they asked for Mark to be moved.

Foster carers

How children become acquainted with you and your family is important. When you meet new children they should experience you as warm and positive and in control of the situation. They are likely to feel apprehensive, confused, troubled and angry. They may need to have some basic physical needs met – to sleep, to have a wash or to eat.

exercise

Think about a child or children recently placed with you. Put yourself in their position. Where had they come from? Why had they been moved? How do you think they were feeling in the first 24 hours? How did you establish a relationship with each one? Is there anything you wish you had done differently?

Ask others – family members, children's social workers, your link workers, children and young people – how they think children saw you when they first came to your home.

Read through Mark's story above. How might he be feeling? How might he behave? If Mark were being placed with you following the disruption of his adoptive placement, how would you introduce yourself to him? How would you explain why he is staying with you? What would you say about the role of your family in his life?

"This is us" album

Children being placed with you can find it helpful to be given a "This is us" album about yourselves. This can be given to them before they come or when they arrive. It has been found to be effective in both planned and emergency foster placements, short and long-term.

The album should give basic information about yourselves that will help children get to know your family and home. Include names and photographs of family members, any pets (and who these belong to) and relatives or important family friends who visit regularly. Photographs of the house, in particular the child's bedroom, the garden, the local school and the family car are also helpful. Put in additional details to bring the family to life – for example, list the names of family members and their interests and hobbies. If there are other children placed with you, add some information (agreed with the child) about him or her. Describe basic family routines, relationships and patterns.

Set out a simple, clear explanation of what fostering families do. You should, of course, also talk with the child about all of this in due course, but a "This is us" album can be a helpful way to welcome a child and to establish a relationship. It is something for the child to keep and to refer to periodically following placement.

Social workers can use a "This is us" album when discussing a planned placement with a child, even if the child is being placed in an emergency or on an immediate basis. Social workers must find a little time, if only on the way to the foster home, to talk about the new family. Children feel far less apprehensive and stressed if they can have at least basic information about a foster family prior to arrival.

Adoptive parents

The need for direct work does not stop when children are finally placed with adoptive parents. It is essential for the new family to show an active interest in the work that has been done so far. Valuing the child's history is linked to valuing the child. Adoption is an exciting new phase, but it has to remain connected to all the other parts of the child's life. Continuing to work with children on their stories and including facts and feelings about their new experiences will help them to keep the pieces together. In time, more memories from the past may surface and be added to the story; often children wait until they feel safe enough to disclose their deepest emotions or to remember being hurt.

Never allow direct work to become a duty or a burden. It should not be like getting homework done – let it grow naturally out of learning to live together, making adjustments, and building trust.

Preparing for the work

Allocating the work

The child's social worker is responsible for planning and undertaking direct work to prepare children for a permanent placement. The child should know the social worker before the work begins.

The practice of allocating direct work to student social workers or sessional workers is sometimes defended with, 'This is better than the alternative which is for it not to happen at all.' Well, it is better than not doing it, but not by much. Children who have had major painful disruptions in their lives need continuity to help them with family transitions to permanence.

In individual cases, of course, it may be beneficial and appropriate for play or family therapists to be in charge of the work. Or, if the social worker is not able to communicate in the child's preferred language, a suitably qualified person would have to be found to interpret or do the work. The child's social worker should make sure that the incoming person's role is clearly understood. In many such cases, joint work to prepare the child for permanence is the best course. On no account should foster carers be burdened with the lead responsibility. However, it is usually appropriate and very effective for social workers to involve foster carers so they can contribute to the work and support the child between sessions.

Gathering and giving information

The quality and outcome of direct work will be significantly affected by the care and attention given to understanding the issues and planning the work with individual children and young people. What will be the aims and objectives? How will progress and results be measured?

The first task is always to gain an informed understanding of the history of the child and the family by reading the child's file carefully, including all medical records. This may mean a half-day spent on one file for an infant, or a week taken to read the complex family history of a twelve-year-old recorded in 12 volumes. A flow chart or chronology of all key events since the child's birth, including the placement history, will help to give an overall picture.

> ## CASE EXAMPLE
> ## SAM
>
> *Sam is a four-year-old boy. His mother, Sarah, is white Welsh. His father, Luke, has white English and black African-Caribbean parents. Sarah and Luke also have a daughter, Sophie, who is six years old; she has lived with her maternal grandmother, Betty, since Sam was born when she was two.*
>
> *Sam has had three foster placements and has lived with both or one of his parents for brief periods. The plan is for Sam to be adopted. Prospective adoptive parents, Sheila and Nigel, have been identified.*

SAM'S FLOW CHART

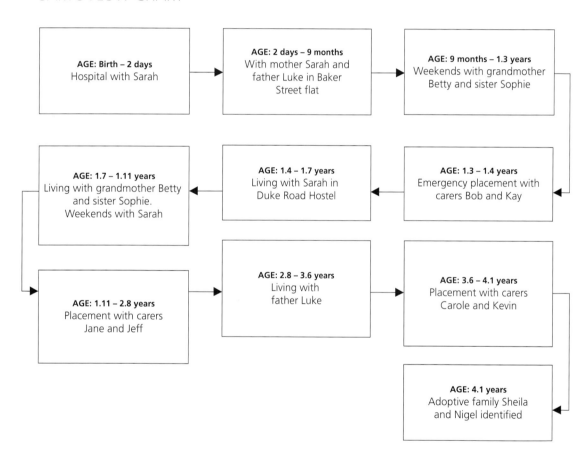

The Victoria Climbié Inquiry Report (Laming, 2003) included a recommendation that 'every child's case file includes, on the inside of the front cover, a properly maintained chronology'. A chronology, whether using text or a flow chart, is not a record of agency involvement – it is a history of all the key events in the child's life from birth to the present.

Other information that should be included in every file is a family tree and a genogram. Chapter 16 gives an example of a genogram for a sibling group. Genograms can be used not only for ease of understanding the information on file, but also in the work with children and young people as described below.

activity

Genogram

Use a small box of male and female characters, which include some duplicates. You will need to have a sound knowledge of the genogram on the file. Introduce the activity to the child by talking about the birth family. You will be making a map of the family using the characters in the box. Invite the child to pick a character for each member of the family and to say why they chose it. This activity can illuminate a child's view of the family, and reveal enjoyable stories, which they do not usually have the opportunity to tell. Try hard not to analyse the choice too much, but simply hear what the child is saying, such as, 'I'm choosing the Mr Sneezy for my brother because he is funny and makes rude noises at the table.' He or she may go on to tell you what happens when the brother makes these noises, and who will tell him off. The genogram is developed as the worker helps the child to place the various characters in their right places on a large sheet of paper.

This activity can help to explain to children why they and a sibling have different birth fathers, or why the child looks similar to some members of the family and not to others, or where absent family members fit into the family network. In time, you could use the same technique to explain about joining a new family where there is already an adopted child in the placement.

Interestingly, teenagers will also join in with this activity – sometimes protesting to begin with – but they can become incredibly intense and precise in the creation of their family.

When you have read the files, set out the child's chronology, made a flow chart and a genogram, you will see whether you understand the background to the whole story. If there are gaps, from where and from whom might you be able to gather missing information?

Background information

- What is the child's precise ethnicity?
- At what ages did the child reach developmental milestones?
- What common childhood diseases has the child had?
- What injuries, illnesses or periods in hospital has the child had?
- What were the child's first words?
- How does the child show affection?
- What does the child do when happy or excited?
- What things is the child wary or afraid of?
- What are the child's comfort strategies/comfort objects?
- Who have been the child's favourite friends?
- What activities and toys does the child like?
- What are the child's favourite and least favourite foods?
- How has the child celebrated birthdays or religious festivals?

- What trips and holidays has the child been on? With whom?

- Who in the extended family has been important to the child?

- What nicknames has the child had?

- What pets has the child known?

- What are the names of the child's teachers, nurseries and schools?

- What have been the child's experiences of faith-based meetings/services been?

- How does the child make people feel?

- How does this child feel about himself or herself?

The Framework for the Assessment of Children in Need and their Families offers a systematic approach for gathering and analysing information about children and their families. This is reproduced below.

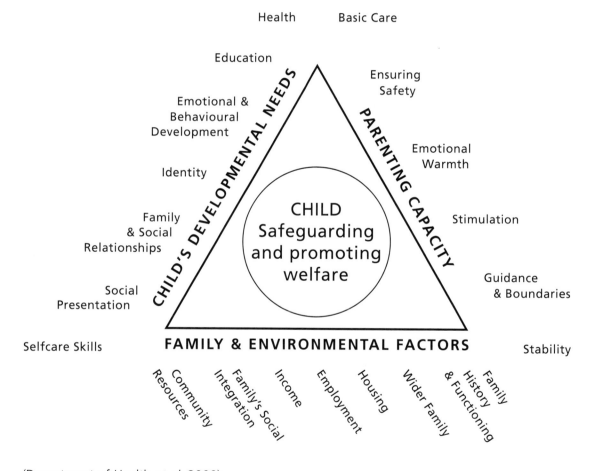

(Department of Health *et al*, 2000)

You may find that a child has experienced significant deficits in parenting and/or in environmental circumstances. In consequence, he or she may have motor or sensory developmental delay or present cognitive or emotional confusion. The National Assembly for Wales' *Practice Guidance on Assessing the Support Needs of Adoptive Families* (2005) references a range of assessment tools which will be helpful in planning preparation for permanence and post-placement support.

Foster carers

Foster carers should be given essential information about every child prior to placement. It may be that in an emergency this is impractical but, even then, the information should be made available within 24 hours. However, carers often report that information about the child's background, health and reasons for coming into foster care are not fully shared with them. This is unjustifiable practice in terms of the welfare of children and placement support, and ultimately is unhelpful for the child.

It is helpful for carers to have (next to the phone) a list of what they consider to be the bare minimum information they need before a child is placed. Whenever possible they should insist that their supervising social worker ensures that the child's worker provides essential information prior to or at the beginning of a placement, followed by full information and discussion of placement aims in the context of the plan for the child.

Foster carers usually spend more time with the child than anyone else – sometimes 24 hours a day. They are in a position to respond to children whenever they are ready to ask questions or talk about confusing matters. Foster carers are an excellent resource for children, but they need the necessary information about the child to enable them to become this excellent resource.

They have to understand what the objectives and key issues are in the ongoing direct work, otherwise the child will inevitably receive conflicting messages. Social workers must work in partnership with foster carers so that carers are very clear about how they are to contribute to the work being planned and undertaken with the child.

Foster carers might:

- help in gathering information;

- reinforce messages and information being given by the social worker;

- support the child through the emotional consequences of the work;

- help the child by building on the social work sessions.

CASE EXAMPLE
SAM

Sam's foster carer, Carole, helped to prepare Sam, who was then just over four years old, for his move to his new adoptive parents.

His social worker was trying to clear up Sam's confusion about the various people he had lived with and how they fitted into his story. She discussed this work with Carole.

Carole asked the social worker for photographs of Sam's birth family and previous foster families. No photograph was available for Sam's emergency placement, so Carole visited the house and took photographs of the carers and Sam's bedroom.

Carole made playhouses out of shoeboxes and stuck a photograph to each one. While she and Sam played with the houses, Carole could go over Sam's story with him and he could ask questions and test out memories.

Adoptive parents

Adoptive parents must have all the information available about their children. All the background information listed above for social workers is also needed by adopters. Prior to placement, adopters can prepare a "This is us" album (see Chapter 5) to use for giving information about themselves to their child.

It is important for adoptive parents to know how children have been prepared for the move and what life story work they will bring. This might include a life story book, a photo album, a cassette or video recording, a memory box and anything else that tells their stories. If children are reluctant to share life story work with their new family, it is best to allow them to go at their own pace and to show it and talk about it when they feel ready.

Children's understanding of the past may still be simplistic or fragmented, and they may still be confused by some events or relationships. As children grow up, their questions can become more searching. If you do not have all the answers there is no harm in saying that you don't know, but that you will try and find out for them. If the child is old enough you can find out together.

Storytelling (in the sense of recounting what has happened) is an essential part of cementing child–parent connections. There are some books available for young adopted children on the theme of 'When I first met you', as an alternative to 'When you were born' but best, of course, is a story written by the adoptive parents for telling and re-telling about meeting their own son or daughter for the first time.

Analysing information

Having background information about a child is a necessary part of preparing for the work. However, it is not the whole. Social workers should assess how this information and how these experiences will affect a child's anticipation of moving to a new permanent family.

Some questions about separations and losses that arise from an initial consideration of Sam's history above are:

- What, if any, effects have two unheralded moves had for Sam?

- How is Sam responding to being separated from each member of his birth family?

- How is Sam responding to being separated from all or any of his previous foster carers?

- What has Sam been told about his future? Who, if anyone, has given him which messages, including all birth family members, foster carers, social workers and other professionals?

- What messages about permanence will Sam need before his move to an adoptive placement?

The information you gather should form part of your analysis of how ready or prepared the child is for becoming part of a new family. How does this child conceptualise family life? How does he or she feel about being emotionally close to others? How does he or she manage separations? How secure do you think the child will be in forming new family relationships?

By the time you are ready to begin direct work, you will have an understanding of the child's:

- development, including sensory and motor skills, cognitive and emotional development;

- health and medical history;

- methods of communication;

- preferred play and leisure activities;

- strategies for feeling safe and secure;

- experiences and expectations of family life;

- experiences and expectations of being parented;

- responses to being separated from family and other important people;

- ways of managing relationships (attachment patterns and behaviours);

- important people in his or her life;

- understanding of what is going to happen in the future.

You will also be able to gauge how the child is likely to view the permanence plan you will be sharing with them.

Planning and managing sessions

Social workers

As you read through the child's history and meet with their family, carers and other professionals, you will be able to move towards identifying the purpose and aims of the work you are planning.

CASE EXAMPLE
A CHRONOLOGY OF MARK'S HISTORY (described in Chapter 5)

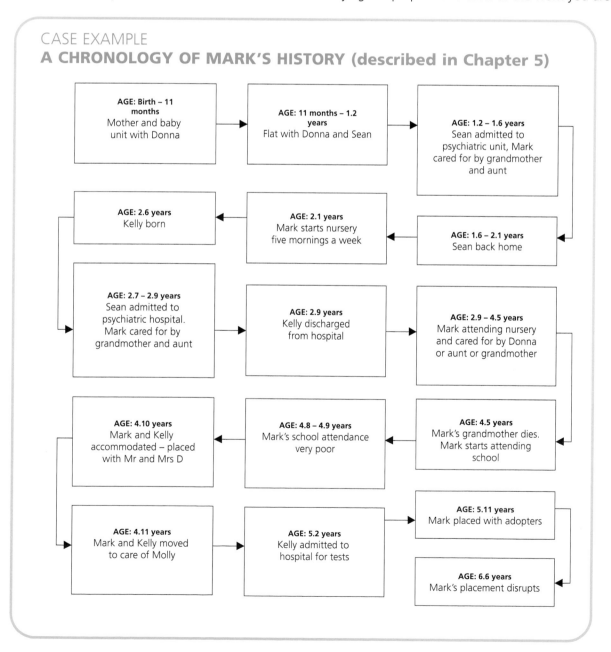

AGE: Birth – 11 months
Mother and baby unit with Donna

AGE: 11 months – 1.2 years
Flat with Donna and Sean

AGE: 1.2 – 1.6 years
Sean admitted to psychiatric unit, Mark cared for by grandmother and aunt

AGE: 2.6 years
Kelly born

AGE: 2.1 years
Mark starts nursery five mornings a week

AGE: 1.6 – 2.1 years
Sean back home

AGE: 2.7 – 2.9 years
Sean admitted to psychiatric hospital. Mark cared for by grandmother and aunt

AGE: 2.9 years
Kelly discharged from hospital

AGE: 2.9 – 4.5 years
Mark attending nursery and cared for by Donna or aunt or grandmother

AGE: 4.10 years
Mark and Kelly accommodated – placed with Mr and Mrs D

AGE: 4.8 – 4.9 years
Mark's school attendance very poor

AGE: 4.5 years
Mark's grandmother dies. Mark starts attending school

AGE: 4.11 years
Mark and Kelly moved to care of Molly

AGE: 5.2 years
Kelly admitted to hospital for tests

AGE: 5.11 years
Mark placed with adopters

AGE: 6.6 years
Mark's placement disrupts

The purpose of direct work with Mark will be to prepare him for a new adoptive placement. The aims might be to:

- help Mark to have a better understanding of:
  - what happened with respect to his mother, his father, his birth sister and his grandmother;
  - how the events set out in Mark's flow chart have affected all these family members, including Mark himself;
  - why Mark had to leave his adoptive family.
- reassure Mark that his sister is safe and will remain safe.
- make Mark more confident about a future permanent placement.

Each of these aims incorporates extremely complex issues. Given Mark's age, the way the sessions are planned will not only have to be appropriate for a six-year-old, but also for a six-year-old who is still actively grieving and is confused and withdrawn.

Later chapters on communicating with children, giving children information, supporting traumatised children, building resilience, and helping children think about a new family will all be relevant for work with Mark.

Timetabling the work

It is essential that the practitioner's caseload allows time for planning and evaluating direct work as well as for the work itself. This should be agreed within the team and with the team manager.

A caseload management system should be in place that reflects departmental recognition of the importance of direct work. Practitioners and managers must lobby for a resourced system instead of struggling to find scarce time for individual cases.

Social workers should talk with the child's foster carers and any other adults concerned to agree a day of the week and time in the day when the sessions will fit into the household routine, and when the child is most likely to have energy and time for the work. Straight after school is a favourite time for social workers but this is also a time when children may be tired and the home is usually busy.

The length of sessions will vary with the age, understanding and circumstances of the child but, in the majority of cases, a session of between one hour and one-and-a-half hours will be appropriate. Some individual sessions may need to be shortened or extended as necessary.

Allow enough time before and after seeing the child to refresh your thoughts and to evaluate and write up sessions. Children and young people's readiness to talk about some of the very sensitive issues addressed in direct work will not necessarily coincide with your timetable. Social workers should try to "seize the moment" if diary commitments allow.

CASE EXAMPLE
NATHAN

Nathan's social worker Beth visited each Wednesday to do life journey work with him. Each session started with a game of pool in the back room.

On the day before the fifth session Beth was told she had to attend court the next day. She was about to telephone Nathan's foster carer to cancel her visit but decided to call round instead to apologise in person.

Nathan had just come in from school and, on Beth telling him that she could not see him the following day, he replied cheerily that it didn't matter as the pool table was set up ready so they could do it today instead.

Beth did not want to disappoint Nathan twice so she stayed. They had one of the best sessions they ever had.

When children have questions they need to be able to ask them at a time that is right for them. The right time for a child may be now – not in four days' time, when you have planned a session. On the other hand, today – a day you have carefully allocated – may be quite the wrong time for the child.

Managers should allow social workers some flexibility to be able to respond to children's needs promptly. This does not necessarily mean discarding diary commitments, nor does it mean being always available, but it does mean a telephone call to the child or foster carer immediately to establish what the child wants to talk about or ask, and then gauging how quickly you need to visit. Social workers should have caseload levels that leave them room to manoeuvre.

If you find you have to change the arrangements you have made to see a child, do this sensitively to fit in with the child's and the family's routines.

Foster carers

Foster carers can contribute to direct work during the daily routine of living together, and by putting aside time for specific activities. Children may also want to raise issues with carers in the ordinary course of family life. These times are likely to occur when other things have to be done – cooking dinner, driving or putting younger children to bed. Carers will need a strategy for being able to listen and answer questions while meeting other demands. It may be that you can give the child some focused initial attention with an assurance that you will give more time later (say when), or perhaps the child is raising something that seems to be of great importance to them and requires your immediate and full attention. For instance, child protection issues frequently come up at the most inconvenient moments.

Adoptive parents

Adoptive parents do not usually plan formalised direct work sessions. Anything connected with a child's or young person's sense of security and continuity will arise periodically in the ordinary course of growing up.

Children are far less likely to consider their adoptive status as a problem if they have always known that they were adopted. Even when children are infants, parents can tell them stories about meeting them for the first time and how they fell in love with them. Adopted children and young people may need their parents to go over parts of their story in different ways as they grow up and can understand things from a new perspective.

CASE EXAMPLE
NATALIE

'I always knew I was adopted – as long as I can remember I knew my mum and dad chose me because my birth mum couldn't look after me. It just wasn't an issue – it's the way it was.

'One day when I was at school, I was playing with my friends in the break and it came up. "Oh," I said, "I'm adopted". There was a bit of a silence and one of my friends said "Oh, I'm sorry". I couldn't understand why she was sorry and I had to ask Mum when I got home.'

Social workers

Prior to the sessions be clear about the arrangements.

- Will the foster carer remind and prepare the child?

- If the sessions are to take place in the foster home, can the carer offer a suitable place for the work?

- Will the foster carer be present, stay in the background, or join in for feedback at the end?

- Will other members of the household be prepared to respect the privacy of the sessions?

- Will a table and chairs be available and comfortable and at the right height? Will there be floor space?

- Will the room be warm/cool enough?

- Will drinks and biscuits be provided or should they be brought in specially?

- Are all the materials needed, for example, paper, pens, scissors, books, puppets, tape recorder, etc, ready in a suitable bag?

- If sessions are to be outside the foster home, how will travel for the child be managed and how will the carers be involved?

The initial session

Discuss the work

In the first session, spend some time talking with the child or young person about why and how you will be spending time together. If the children are older than infants, check out key background information with them. Taking into account their age and understanding, flag up some of the issues you may be covering in future sessions.

- Explain your role.

- Make it clear that the time you will spend together can be used to consider any aspect of their life with birth family and with foster carers.

- Reassure the child that she will have choices in the process.

- Give the child plenty of opportunities to ask you questions at every stage.

- Explain how some information can be kept confidential, but why other information may have to be shared.

Establish the contract

Again, depending upon the child's understanding, draw up a contract together to include:

- the number of sessions you agree on;

- how long each session will be;

- the dates when you will meet (the child could have or make a diary);

- where you will work (office, foster home, family centre);

- who might join in (for example, the foster carer or a sibling);

- who the information will be shared with (foster carers, prospective families, other social workers) and what it will be used for;

- who the child might want to talk to after sessions.

Develop awareness of the child's perceptions

Try to gain an idea of the mindset the child is bringing to the work you are planning.

- How does the child understand the issues to be addressed and who has influenced this understanding?

- How is the child likely to view you and working together?

- How might the child's history and experiences impact on his or her sense of "family" and "permanence"?

- What and who are the child's main concerns?

Ending the first session

Before you leave, go over the main points again and write down what you have agreed. Give the child a card with the date, time and place of the next meeting. Following the initial session, record the work in a dedicated folder to keep with the child's file. Discuss and refine the direct work plan with your manager. Agree the timetable and resources you will need. Confirm in writing the plan for future sessions with the child and the child's carers and, having regard for the child's wishes about confidentiality, outline to the carers the issues you will be covering in the various sessions.

Foster carers

Hosting the initial session

The foster carer should welcome the worker into the house and help to settle the child and the worker into the room to be used. The carer should stay in the house throughout the social worker's visit and, together with the child, say goodbye when the worker leaves.

Following the initial session

The child might be feeling upset at the end of the session – he or she may want some time to be alone, or need to spend some time just with their carer. It may be good to have a drink and a snack together and to share an activity the child enjoys.

The child may want to talk there and then or later, perhaps before bedtime. It is important, however, not to put pressure on the child to talk about how the session went, but to record any reactions the child has in the foster home, and to tell the social worker of these.

Social workers
Subsequent sessions

Before each subsequent session

- Re-read your notes from previous sessions. Make a note of any new thoughts and questions you have.

- Ensure you are up to date with what has been happening since you last saw the child. Check with the foster carers or other professionals.

- Make a note of any particular issues that are emerging or need addressing with the child.

- If you have not yet been able to discuss the work with your manager, make a date now.

- Consider whether the venue you have used is appropriate for the next or subsequent sessions.

- Note the resources you will need to have in place for planned activities.

During each subsequent session

- Arrive in good time and be fully prepared. Clear your mind of other concerns, no matter how pressing they are.

- Turn off your mobile phone.

- Start each session by re-visiting with the child what happened last time you were together. Is there anything in particular he or she remembers? How does the child feel about this now?

- Allow the child to tell you what, if anything, has happened since the last session that has a bearing on today.

- Observe and listen carefully. What thoughts might be behind the child's play, expressions or verbal communication?

- Do you need to change the activities or allow more time for free play? What do you aim to achieve by this?

- Towards the end of the session, start to draw the activities to a timely close.

- Recap on any particular points you want to reinforce with the child.

- Structure the closing period to enable the child to be calm and ready for the rest of the day.

After each session

- Reflect on what has happened during the session. What understanding did you and the child take away from the activities?

- What significance has the session had for preparing the child for permanence?

- How did the child seem? What emotions were apparent and in what connection?

- Make full notes on the same day if possible – if not, then no later than the next day.

- Note any misconceptions the child continues to have about the past, the present situation and plans for the future. Note any positive changes in these perceptions.

- Think about the play and communication techniques that were used. What worked best in terms of the aims of the work? What worked less well?

- Arrange to talk with any other people/agencies necessary to progress the work.

- Make a note of what action you need to take before the next session. Consider how the child behaved when you parted – if you think he or she might have questions or emotional difficulties arising from the work, let the foster carers know without breaching the confidentiality arrangements you have made.

Foster carers

Before each session

Carers can help to support the child by asking whether there are any things the child would like to do to help prepare for the next session.

During each session

Other children in the placement should not be allowed to interrupt. They may feel envious of the "special time" a foster child is having – it will be helpful if the carer can involve them in a game of their own.

After each session

Carers should have access to the same or similar materials used by the child and social worker so that they can continue with the work between visits if appropriate.

Carers should establish whether there are any tasks the social worker would like them to undertake, and make sure that time is set aside to discuss progress before the next session.

Child protection issues

Preparation for permanence work and for therapy should complement each other; both should support healing and move the child towards feeling safe in a permanent new family.

However, very often the extent of past abuse will not have been established. There may be grounds for suspicion but no disclosure or available evidence. If this is the case, it is unwise to raise the issue early on in the work.

Whom do children confide in? They most often feel able to disclose or to allude to abuse when they are with an adult whom they have learned to trust and who makes them feel safe. Direct work with children can often offer the safe and empowering environment in which they feel able to talk about abusive experiences.

If a child you are to work with is known to have been physically or perhaps sexually abused, it can be helpful to say early on that you are aware of this, otherwise the child can spend some uncomfortable time wondering whether you know, and what to say about it.

You can say something like: 'I know a bit about what has happened to you' (for example, that Granddad hurt you badly). 'We can talk about it during these times together, if that feels alright for you.'

Be clear that you do not necessarily expect to talk about the abuse – it is their choice, at all times.

Find out who else, if anyone, is offering therapeutic work in connection with the abuse – you should not be replacing or duplicating therapy.

CASE EXAMPLE
BETHAN

Bethan had been sitting at the kitchen table, with her social worker, Kanu, for the beginning part of the afternoon. They had begun to draw a visual pathway of Bethan's early life at home with her mother. Following the session, they went into another room to join Sarah, the foster carer. Sarah had been removing her nail polish.

Bethan began to show real signs of distress. Fresh from her life journey work, Bethan was encountering the distinctive smell of nail polish remover, which she associated with her mother. Memories of being abused by her mother flooded in. For the first time, Bethan talked to Kanu and Sarah about her distressing past.

For some children it may be much easier to use non-verbal communication to disclose abuse.

CASE EXAMPLE
CHLOE

Chloe was talking with her social worker, Kate, about the people she would go to for certain things – she would go to her grandma for a hug, to her mother if she wanted food, and to her "Uncle" Barry if she wanted to play with the animals. Kate asked Chloe about these animals. The play materials in the room included some animal glove puppets. Chloe chose the elephant. She described how Uncle Barry asked her to stroke the elephant's trunk; she used the puppet to show that he would turn the pockets of his trousers inside out to be the elephant's ears and that his penis was the elephant's trunk.

Responding to a disclosure

Children often present information a bit at a time – perhaps hinting about an experience at first and later going on to talk in more detail. Make sure the child knows you are listening. He or she will be alert to how you are receiving the information. It might be helpful to sit down so you are nearer the child's height, and not to change position too much or move about the room during the child's disclosures.

Social workers must be clear about agency procedures and the provisions of *Working Together to Safeguard Children* (Department of Health *et al*, 1999) in the event of a disclosure of abuse. Social workers, foster carers and adoptive parents should have a clear and shared understanding of how to respond to disclosures.

Do not lead the child into elaborating too much at the time of the initial disclosure. Your aim will be for the child to feel heard and reassured, but not to elicit full information. A prolonged discussion might impair any future evidence.

Good practice points

1. Do not panic. Do not react with horror. Do not show how upset you are. It may be appropriate to let the child know that you are finding what he or she is telling you difficult because you care about what has happened to them, but do not take over the agenda.

2. Take what the child says seriously, even if the allegation involves someone you know and trust. Children have been abused while being looked after and all disclosures should be taken seriously.

3. Try to remember exactly what the child says.

4. Do not be drawn into promising confidentiality. Explain clearly that you have a responsibility to keep the child safe and to keep other children safe. This means you must tell the social worker/your manager about it. For smaller children, use simpler concepts, such as that unhappy things need to be passed on to someone who can sort things out.

5. Acknowledge that asking for advice or talking about abuse can be very difficult – reassure the child that he or she has done the right thing in telling you and that you will help.

6. Do not put words into the child's mouth. Long pauses can be difficult, but listen to the silence.

7. Keep an open mind and do not jump to conclusions.

8. Do not attempt to question or interview the child. Let them find their own words to describe their experiences. Do not ask the child to repeat anything.

9. Tell the child what you intend to do next. This should be to contact the child's social worker/your team manager now. Explain that this person will be able to arrange things so that the child (and others) will be safe. Tell the child when you have done this and what will happen now.

10. Immediately contact the social services (your manager if you are a social worker) or the police and explain your concerns. Ideally, follow this up in writing within 48 hours.

11. As soon as you can, record carefully what you and the child said to each other. Use the exact words if you can remember them. Stick to facts – do not record your opinions.

12. On no account contact or confront the alleged abuser – no matter who they are.

The following is an extract from the Welsh Assembly Government's *Safeguarding Children: Working together for positive outcomes* (2004), which offers some useful pointers to good practice.

All those working with children and families should…

- Be familiar with and follow their organisation's procedures and protocols for promoting and safeguarding the welfare of children, and know whom to contact in the organisation to express concerns about a child's welfare.

- Refer any concern about child abuse or neglect to social services or the police.

- Remember that an allegation of child abuse or neglect may lead to a criminal investigation. Whenever someone encounters a case which constitutes, or may constitute, a criminal offence against a child, they should always inform the police at the earliest opportunity and should not do anything that may jeopardise police enquiries and investigation, such as asking a child leading questions or attempting to investigate the allegations of abuse.

- Communicate with the child in a way that is appropriate to their age, understanding and preference. This is especially important for disabled children and for children whose preferred language is not English. The nature of this communication will also depend on the substance and seriousness of the concerns and you may require advice from social services or the police to ensure that neither the safety of the child nor any subsequent investigation is jeopardised. Where concerns arise as a result of information given by a child it is important to reassure the child but not to promise confidentiality.

- Record all concerns, discussions about the child, decisions made and the reasons for those decisions.

Communicating with children

General principles

When embarking on direct work with children, give the message that it is alright for them to ask you any questions they may have and that you will do your very best to answer.

We, as adults, often think that a child understands what we are saying because we have used language that is clear to us. Throughout our relationships with children, however, we should bear in mind that our phrases and words may be unfamiliar to them.

We should always:

- be aware of the individual child's preferred ways of communicating;

- reflect back what the child is saying;

- ask open questions;

- remember that we can all have contradictory views and feelings within even short periods of time (don't say, 'But you said…', but rather, 'I think sometimes you feel one way and sometimes another…');

- try to understand what meaning a child is giving to the words you are both using – ask them;

- try not to seem anxious: children will remember what it was like being with you and talking with you. They will value your openness, trustworthiness and reliability.

The child's preferred language/means of communication

The person undertaking direct work and guided play should be able to use the preferred language or means of communication of the child or young person. If the child's social worker is not able to do so, then another suitably qualified person should be allocated or commissioned to undertake the work. For example, if a disabled child communicates significantly more effectively with a specific person, then that person and the child's social worker should work together with the child.

A time and a place

There is a well-established tradition of social workers taking children to fast food outlets for discussions. Undeniably, this offers some benefits – children will often want to go, enjoying the food and atmosphere – but the drawbacks are noise, time pressures and distractions. On the whole, a walk or a quieter venue will allow for better communication.

Children may find it helpful to know that at certain times of each week (or during the day if you are a carer) you are going to be available. Many children have no experience at all of adults giving attention to them and may need encouragement to respond. Sometimes children find it easier to talk while something else is going on. You could say something like: 'I am cooking dinner' or 'I have to keep my eyes on the road, but can chat if you'd like'. We also have to be prepared for children to choose their own times to communicate – sometimes just when they are supposed to be going to sleep, or when guests are about to arrive, or when the social worker has to attend a meeting.

Verbal communication

Looked after children and young people tend to meet many adults who ask them many questions. Some children will have had a number of social workers, and this can mean having to retell their story repeatedly, which can be wearisome and distressing. New social workers and carers should demonstrate by listening and positively responding that it will be worthwhile to trust once more.

'A nine-year-old told me that 'Before a social worker starts telling me important things about my life they should at least get to know me.' This reminded me that the first stage of communicating is listening.

'As a social worker I wasn't trained in communicating with children. I learnt about advocacy, empowerment and children's rights, but it seemed to be taken for granted that the art of communication was a skill that I already possessed. Communicating with children, from my own experience, is a most complex and demanding area of work. Strategies employed to share information, give explanations and elicit thoughts and feelings have to be developed over time, and inspiration must be allowed to come from a variety of sources.'

(Personal communication from child's social worker)

exercise

Think of a time when you were a child and wanted very much to talk to an adult about something. What factors made it easier or more difficult to start?

Listening to children/talking with children

- Listen patiently to what the child or young person is saying, even though you may consider it to be unrelated or misconceived. The child will be imparting what, from his or her perspective, is relevant and real. Indicate simple acceptance, not necessarily agreement, by nodding or perhaps injecting an occasional 'mm-hmm' or 'I see'.

- Ask open questions. These often start with 'Tell me about…school/living here/last week…' Open questions work well when you are getting to know the child, at the beginning of a session during or following free play or if you feel the work is getting "blocked".

- Getting "blocked" describes times when the conversation is repetitive, circular or stalled. You can try saying: 'I notice that when we talk about this you often say "so what" or "I'm not going to" (or whatever the young person says to block the discussion). What else could happen? How can you and I change things so that we can think about this differently?'

- Try to understand the feelings the child is expressing. You can ask at times how the child feels about what is being discussed.

- Restate some of the child's phrases so the child can elaborate or re-phrase, if helpful. Do not put words into the child's mouth or interpret what he or she is saying. Simply act as a mirror – reflect back.

- Allow time for the child to talk without interruption if he or she wants to. Take your cue from the child about when to join in and when to stop.

- Try to get clarification when this is appropriate – 'So from what you just said, am I right in thinking that…?' or 'So how did you feel about that?'

- Use closed questions when you are aiming to elicit answers to specific questions. Closed questions require answers like 'yes', 'no' or 'because…' You can also use closed questions when a child or young person is avoiding or "waffling". Bear in mind that closed questions can be threatening, so use them sparingly. Do not use them routinely in your work with the child or at the start of a session.

- Listen out for what is not being said. For instance, a young person with little experience of nurturing care may describe school life, family events and friendships without reference to emotions.

- If the child "slips in" a piece of information or a thought that is important and quickly moves on to something else, you can easily return to it with a simple 'I heard you say…just now', or 'What was it you just said about…?'

- If the child asks for your views, be honest but sensitive in your reply.

- Do not talk about yourself. Do not relate what the child is saying to your own experiences ('I remember when something similar happened to me…'). If you have genuinely been in a similar situation (for example, in care) it may be helpful in terms of unblocking a piece of work to use this, but do it with caution, be clear why you are doing it and what, in your view, will be gained by it. It is generally not a useful tool for establishing a relationship with a child. Giving a child or young person sensitive personal information passes on a responsibility the child could probably do without. If things get difficult between you, the information could be used by the child to make you feel uncomfortable.

- Do not get emotionally involved yourself in the child's story.

- Try simply to understand. Analysis comes later.

Tolerating silences

Silences can indicate:

- boredom;

- embarrassment;

- not knowing or understanding what's going on;

- not knowing what to expect;

- "sizing" you up;

- "winding" you up;

- repressing strong emotions;

- thinking;

- being overwhelmed by the situation;

- wanting to be somewhere else (football game/favourite TV programme);

- getting prepared to tell you something;

- remembering things that happened last time;

- avoiding discussion;

- being tired.

CASE EXAMPLE
PAUL

Rhodri, Paul's social worker, arrived for the third session of direct work with five-year-old Paul, who was to be adopted by his foster carers. Paul was reticent and slumped in the chair. 'What's up, Paul?' asked Rhodri. 'I'm too tired,' said Paul, 'I'm too tired to tell.' Rhodri sat with Paul and watched television with him, both drinking juice. After a comfortable time in silence together, Rhodri said goodbye and returned the following week.

It can sometimes feel awkward for the worker (and indeed the child) to tolerate silence. However, silent times can be thought provoking and can provide space to choose subjects and words with care.

Pacing/emotional listening

Pacing is a technique of acknowledging a child's emotions – of helping them to be in touch with and express feelings – without being overwhelmed by them. Sometimes, in order for us to feel emotionally "heard", we need the other person to respond to our emotional high with an increased momentum of their own. What then often happens in an argument is that each person tops the other's emotional level so the tension escalates. In the context of "emotional listening", the technique is the opposite.

The young person may provoke you initially to match the pace and energy he or she is using to express intense feelings. You should not match feeling with feeling, but rather simply heighten the pace at which you talk and exaggerate your facial expressions while you listen and respond. Then quite quickly reduce your pace in stages, with the aim of helping to decelerate tension.

This technique is the opposite of having an argument – each of your communications should be aimed at having slightly less momentum than that of the child. If this is effective, the child will gradually relax without feeling unheard.

exercise

Think of a time when you were very angry with another person and ready for an argument but the other person persisted in being calm and disengaged from your anger. How did this affect your feelings and behaviours?

Checking your assumptions

Sometimes communication is difficult because you and the child may have a very different understanding of family life.

CASE EXAMPLE
MARK

'No matter what I tried, I couldn't get it though to him. Also, I couldn't understand what he was on about most of the time. It was like there was a computer and we had different disks in. I had to explain the simplest things – for instance, about why it was important for me and the family that he joined us for breakfast in the mornings.

'I eventually found out that he'd never eaten breakfast, not with anyone, just a bag of crisps on the way to school.'

(Mark's foster carer)

CASE EXAMPLE
CERI

When Margaret took over the case and met Ceri, aged 13, Ceri made it clear that she was not happy. She said very little but sat, arms and legs crossed, looking out of the window at the apparently interesting car park. After some time, during which Margaret had tried every way she knew to ease the atmosphere, Ceri frowned at Margaret and pointed out that she was too old to be her social worker.

Margaret was a bit taken aback (and perturbed that she was apparently entering her dotage!). She agreed that she was older than Ceri's previous social worker. Ceri became upset. Margaret knew that Ceri had liked and trusted her previous social worker and hadn't wanted to lose her. It became apparent that this wasn't an age issue; it was a person issue.

PREPARING CHILDREN FOR PERMANENCE

Non-verbal communication

Neilson (1973) says, 'In our culture, adults tend to distrust communication that is not verbal and will often seek verbal confirmation of information received on a non-verbal level. A child, however, does not always have the words to describe his feelings accurately, even if he recognises what they are.'

Eye contact

Eye contact can sometimes be uncomfortable for children when they are telling you something that is difficult for them. They may opt for situations where eye contact is avoidable but where you are not easily able to leave. Car journeys and meal preparation times are classic examples. You will need to vary your approach, however, as eye contact can be important.

CASE EXAMPLE
PIPPA

'When Pippa first came she didn't help out with anything. She mainly wanted to watch television or read in her room. Gradually, she started helping with the animals and she used to like feeding them. One day we were out with the dogs in the fields and she stopped by this big tree trunk that was on the ground and she said, 'Sit down, there's something I want to tell you.' Well, she started talking about her mother and about all these terrible things she used to do to Pippa. She'd been badly sexually abused and she was telling me all about it. She'd never said a word to anyone before.

'I wanted to make it as OK as I could for her to talk about it so I sat still. I thought she might prefer it if there was no eye contact so I looked at the ground while she talked. After a bit she stopped and said to me, 'I'm talking to you, the least you can do is look at me. I'm talking to you!' Of course, I felt awful but I said, 'I'm sorry, Pippa, I am listening very carefully. I thought you might find it a bit uncomfortable for me to be looking at you, but I'd prefer to really. I am listening.' Pippa was all right with that and she went on talking. She talked for two hours. I put my arm around her shoulders as we walked home.'

(Pippa's foster carer)

What this foster carer did was just right. She knew Pippa well and so took the view that avoiding eye contact would be more comfortable for her. When it was clear that this was not the case, she quickly explained, apologised, and maintained good eye contact from then on.

Generally, your body language should be "neutral". Whether sitting or standing, half-turn or face towards the child or young person. Do not fidget. Do not look at your watch. If there is a clock in the room and you need to look at it occasionally, do so unobtrusively. Be aware of your facial expression.

If you and the child are engaged in an activity and the child stops to talk, then stop as well. If the child continues with the activity then you should too, but concentrate on the child rather than the activity.

The general rule is not to touch the child unless this has become an accepted part of your relationship (for example, if you are a foster carer). If the child becomes distressed, and it is compatible with your safe caring strategy for that child, you can offer a hug or an arm around the shoulders, or simply hold the child's hand.

Support

Some children and young people do not know how to respond to praise or support – many will be unused to it, and some with low self-esteem may find it hard to accept. Most children, however, can appreciate a non-verbal "well done" in the form of a "thumbs up" or a smile and a nod. As you get to know the individual child better, you will be able to gauge what works best for them.

Play techniques

If direct work is "play with a purpose", then it follows that the worker or carer and the child will play together in ways that are age-appropriate for the individual child. Adults may find the prospect of plasticine, puppets or imaginative play rather daunting if they have not played "for fun" for a while. It helps to practise playing with the materials you are proposing to use. Play on your own or with other adults and children before beginning direct work. You will probably find that you enjoy some sorts of play more than others – capitalise on this and have fun, but also have a go at those techniques that feel less natural to you.

You may find that the children you will be working with are unused to play and games, so it is a good idea to explore how a child feels about a particular game before you begin.

activity

Feelings faces

Happy

Sad

Angry

Scared

Feelings faces can be used either on their own or in conjunction with other play techniques to check out how a child is feeling on the day about the current session, or about the issues being raised. They can also be used to help a child consider how other people might have felt or be feeling. You can make a whole range of feelings faces or can buy ready-made cards or finger puppets from educational play stores and catalogues.

Comfort *et al* (2004) advise that the play of toddlers and pre-schoolers teaches them to communicate, to share and to negotiate. 'Play also serves as a means to express ideas and feelings while solving problems. It provides a safe space for risking and for trying something new. Children who come into care may not usually have had early play opportunities.'

Helping children to play

- Introduce play times gently and gradually.

- Investing money in expensive toys is less important than investing time.

- Help children feel safe in their play – play is about exploring and risking.

- Provide many odds and ends of materials (such as empty kitchen or loo rolls, old phone directories, newspapers, magazines, catalogues, plastic bowls, bottles, wooden spoons, fabric pieces, sticky-tape, empty boxes, ribbons, string).

Comfort *et al* add: 'Children need to have adults around while they play so that the adult can organise materials, activities, ideas and limits that enable children to play safely and happily. Some aspects of play that may not work too well include:

- Surprises [which] are rarely good things for children in care…children in care often "lose it" when something is not predictable.

- Other children may not like to play with children who play too repetitively and who never share – which sometimes happens for children in care. They can repeat their play and stay with the same toy because it is comforting and safe.

- Messy play can be quite problematic. Many children in care were severely punished for getting dirty or for wasting things. Sexually abused children often have quite significant issues around messy substances.

- Unbeknown to a parent, carers, teacher or another child, particular toy or story or item of play may have specific meaning to a child in care. The child may appear to overreact by acting out in an unpredictable, sometimes unmanageable fashion. A quiet time with an adult is much more effective management than is punishment when this happens.'

Giving children information and undertaking life journey work

'Children can accept anything if you tell them in the right way. It's the grown-ups who find things difficult to accept.'
Adoptive mother

Children have a right to information about their lives and will need the person sharing it with them to be clear and unambiguous, allowing them time to integrate it with what they already know and to ask further questions.

CASE EXAMPLE
SIOBHAN

Siobhan's father was in prison for physically abusing her and attempting to suffocate her with a pillow when she was three. Siobhan was now eight and had been living with her current foster carers for four years: she would be staying with them until she was 16. Siobhan had recently started to talk with them about her memories of being beaten and nearly suffocated, and so her social worker, Val, started to work with her about her experiences. Siobhan wanted to know why her father had hated her so much and had hit her so hard that she had to go to hospital. Why had he nearly killed her?

Val's aims were to help Siobhan understand that her father was very wrong to have treated her like that, but also to explain that he was struggling with losing his job, not having enough money for the family and not coping at all.

Val talked with Siobhan about how most people, when things go wrong, are able to get help from friends and professionals and can usually manage to get by. But some people become overwhelmed by everything that is going wrong – they can get physically ill, or they can get very depressed. When this happens a person can drink so much alcohol that they become confused and sometimes violent.

Val was concerned about telling Siobhan how her father nearly suffocated her with a pillow – she was worried that it might make Siobhan fearful of her bedroom and of going to sleep. She talked this over with her manager and the foster carer. It was agreed that Siobhan should be told accurately what had happened but that her father had used a cushion from his own room. This would describe the incident honestly while distancing it from Siobhan's present life.

Giving difficult information

To make difficult information as tolerable as possible for children:

- use language they understand and be honest with them – if you don't know details, say so;

- give information in context;

- make it clear you are not expecting them to react in any particular way;

- give them time to feel and express emotions safely with you at the time and in the next and following few days;

- give the message that you will be able to help them manage and express their emotions in ways they can handle;

- help them feel able to ask you any questions they want.

When you are working with children, try to give them ownership of the information being introduced. Link it to the memories and knowledge the child already has. Help children to consider how the others involved may have experienced these things or what their perceptions might have been. Let the child or young person have some say in the timing and manner of receiving information. Some will want to "get it all over with" in one go but need time later on to question and discuss. Others will want information in "bite-size" pieces.

CASE EXAMPLE
KAYLEIGH

Kayleigh was six and was not always sure if her social worker, Ravinder, would be able to answer all the questions she wanted to ask. Sometimes she did not want to ask questions about her life because the answers might make her feel unhappy, and often it was nice just to talk about school. Kayleigh also felt uncomfortable about asking questions in front of other people.

She and Ravinder thought about it and both felt it would be a good idea to have appointed times when they could talk to each other about anything at all – including her adoption.

They chose a good place – a quiet part of the garden under a tree. They devised "sweet swaps". The rule was that when Kayleigh took a chocolate she had to ask a question. If she offered Ravinder a chocolate, it meant that Ravinder had to reply. The questions could be about anything at all. Kayleigh began with: 'What is your favourite colour?', which established a pattern, and they went on to talk about her past and where her family was now. Ravinder was invited to suggest how Kayleigh might handle certain difficult situations. After each session Kayleigh was able to come away with some resolution and a degree of calm.

Life journey work

One of the most effective ways of helping children and young people reconnect with their early years is through life journey work.

- Life journey work means exploring co-operatively with a child or young person the story of his or her life so far. (The phrase "life story work" has been taken by a few children to mean just that – a story, not a history – and so we refer to "life journey work" here.)

- The importance of life journey work is the work itself – one or more adults helping a child to know and understand all aspects of his or her life to date.

- There may be an end product – a life journey book, a memory box, a video or audio tape – but, as important as these are, it is the quality of the process and the development of a child's personal understanding and confidence in the company of a trusted adult that are critical.

- Some children who have had many moves have experienced their lives only as a series of episodes, each one requiring them to adapt to a new setting. Life journey work can help children to see their lives as a continuum.

- Life journey work places the child at the centre of the adult's attention – a new experience for many looked after children. It allows the child's world, from the child's perspective, to predominate.

- Children who have been separated from their birth families and other carers who were important to them have missed out on being able to recall experiences, process feelings, confirm events and align perceptions with the help of constant adults. Life journey work gives children's history back to them. The past can be contextualised. Interconnecting relationships can be explored. Reasons for moves and separations can be questioned. 'Who am I?' and 'How did I get here?' can be answered.

Living with uncertainty

Planning and court processes sometimes keep permanence options for children open for a long time, and in some cases for too great a proportion of children's lives.

> Interviewer: What was the waiting like?
>
> Girl: Terrible
>
> Interviewer: Terrible? What was terrible about it?
>
> Girl: I wait, I wait, I wait…
>
> Interviewer: Yes…
>
> Girl: I wait for the telephone to ring every day
>
> Interviewer: And no news?
>
> Girl: No news…until my fifth year (of waiting)
>
> (from Thomas *et al*, 1999, p 40)

If we do not know when situations are going to change, or what will be decided, we should be honest in saying that we do not know. We can, however, be clear about the things we do know.

We can usually help by offering children small steps of certainty. This involves talking to them about events in the immediate future – a meeting or a contact visit.

exercise

Think about some situations or events you have encountered that prolonged uncertainty for children or added to their confusion rather than alleviating it.

Looking back, how do you think you might have used direct work to help these children ?

Tracking past events

Workers can use simple diagrams to mark key events and movements in a child's life. Children will often find it simpler and more logical to work back through time, starting from where they are now. It may be helpful for the worker to use pencil when tracking a particular change or move, and to invite the child to go over it in ink or crayons.

Below are two examples of graphic representations of events in Mark's life (see Mark's story in Chapter 5).

Mark's life graph

1998	**1 March – born at 7:00am in hospital. Then lived with birth mother Donna in mother and baby unit**
1999	
2000	**Lived in flat at 11 River Road with Donna and Sean** Sean admitted to hospital
2001	**Second birthday with Donna and Sean**
2002	**Kelly born on 18 June** Sean admitted to hospital. Mark cared for by grandmother and aunt Susan
2003	**Started going to Riverbank School** **Went to live at Molly's house with Kelly** **Fifth birthday party at Molly's house**

Bold entries are those Mark was happy to talk about.

Light entries are those the worker will discuss when Mark is more receptive.

Life journey work tracks histories with all their integral elements. It often makes sense to incorporate a visual representation of the child's life journey. This can be any sort of illustrated progression – a pathway, a river, a train, or a series of boxes, or a journey laid out as a board game.

Birthday Cakes – Mark's details		Sam's footprints		
	6th Birthday **With adopters**		**4**	New mum and dad
	5th Birthday **Living with Molly**		3–4	Living with carers Carol and Kevin
	4th Birthday Living with grandmother		2–3	Living with dad and Luke
	3rd Birthday Living with mum Donna and Kelly (6 months old)		2–2	Living with carers Jane and Jeff
	2nd Birthday Just started nursery Living with mum Donna		1–2	Living sometimes with grandmother, sometimes with Sarah
			1	Lived a month with carers Bob and Kay
	1st Birthday Living in flat with mum Donna and dad Sean		9 mths –1	Living with Sarah, weekends with grandmother and Sophie
			Birth– 9 mths	Living with Sarah and dad Luke

You can usefully begin life journey work by illustrating only a part of the child's life, although you may eventually chart all of it. Start with a section of the journey that is fairly non-controversial – perhaps the recent past leading to the present day, or another period when the child has been settled. This will get you working together on the idea of a journey; the child can draw or write or talk about any aspect of the period under review.

The child's thoughts and feelings about various events can be depicted by adding drawings or stickers such as "feelings faces" or weather symbols (sunny/rainy/stormy) next to the life path. If the child likes using play figures or puppets, you can photograph them, and the child can then cut them out and glue them on.

Your joint exploration of any period of the child's life can lead to other more focused work on points arising from the child's experiences at that time. This can involve obtaining more information (photographs/anecdotes/names of friends) or clarifying certain events (information on file/checking out with other people) or helping the child recognise and express feelings associated with that period.

If you are making a book and the child is uncomfortable with writing, it is important not to make them struggle. You can, if asked, help them to correct their work. Some children will enjoy talking into a dictaphone and you can write it up for them afterwards. The important thing is for the pages to be a reflection of the work you are doing jointly – not to be perfect.

'It may also be worth considering using a ring binder if a book is being produced, so that children can edit bits in or out. For example, a child's emotional response to a particular adult in their life may be affected by current issues that they are discussing. This is especially relevant for children who have been sexually assaulted and have not disclosed at the time of their life story work. There may be a picture of them with the perpetrator in their book. Whilst the child may at some point in the future like to reclaim positive feelings they had for their parent who sexually offended them, it may be that at this point they are unable to experience positive feelings.'

(from Ryan and Walker, 2003, p 17)

Healing from trauma

Children who have experienced trauma in their past need careful and sensitive help to support progressive healing. Children who have known domestic violence or abuse are likely at some level to expect that this is what happens in families. The prospect of a move to a new unknown family may lead them to regress to well-tried protective or survival behaviours, which can be profoundly confusing and worrying for carers and adopters. These can include:

- Distancing behaviours

  - being dirty and smelly

  - being rude

  - not accepting affection or nurture

  - refusing to abide by household rules

  - screaming

  - talking all the time

  - running away

- Submissive behaviours

  - being sexually inviting

  - responding sexually to affection or nurture

  - being exaggeratedly helpful or good

  - having extremely low expectations of self and others

- "Distancing behaviours", abuse

  - being unable or unwilling to sleep or go to bed/be bathed/accept food /be photographed

  - not changing clothes

  - being physically distant from others

- Blocking behaviours

  - dissociating present experiences from the past

  - not being able to tolerate the feelings associated with the abuse – guilt, shame, fear

  - sleeping too much

  - being hyperactive

Even after children have been placed in safety, any new stressful situation can mean that they feel the need to go back into survival mode. This is how they have managed in the past and this will be their resource now. For some children, however, such behaviour can become habitual – no longer linked to traumatic events, or even to times of stress or the fear of hurt. It can become their everyday conduct and means of communication.

When you encounter these distancing, submissive and dissociating behaviours in your direct work with children, establishing a working, empathetic relationship is going to be a struggle. Yet if children are to have the best chance of not only surviving in a family, but thriving in a family, direct work to reduce the effects of post-traumatic stress disorder will be an important part of their healing. Post-traumatic stress disorder is a syndrome of adaptive behaviours that are evolved by individuals to help them to survive terror.

The practice points described in Chapter 5 about establishing a relationship with the child and explaining your role will be especially important for traumatised children. They may need you regularly to repeat what the arrangements are. They will also need the contract about working together to be very clear. Your approach to the work should be informed by detailed knowledge about the abuse – as a simple example, a child may experience your saying that he or she is safe with you as a frightening statement because the abuser used similar words.

Children should know what their options are. Can they take time out from direct work or stop if they need to?

Establish a safe practice/safe caring strategy with your manager or your supervising social worker or the child's social worker. Do not deviate from it. The strategy should include always having another adult in the house during direct work, keeping the door of the room in which you are working with the child ajar, and keeping careful records about how you and the child interacted in each session/activity.

Although direct work in preparing children for permanence can be a most valuable contribution to the process of recovery from trauma, it is not a substitute for expert therapeutic support. Children who have been systematically abused and frightened are entitled to specialist help. Social work practitioners and foster carers will then contribute to a supportive, but irreplaceable role.

Elements of direct work with children and young people who are healing from neglect or abuse will include:

- giving additional information to the child about the neglect or abuse. Children can find the absence of information more frightening than knowing what occurred;

- answering the question: 'Why me?' Many children who have been abused or severely neglected think that they were in some way to blame – that they invited the abuse, deserved to be punished or failed to protest sufficiently. Children should be helped to understand that abuse or neglect is always the responsibility of the perpetrator. Children cannot control the situation when adults misuse their powerful position;

- helping children and young people recognise their feelings and express them in ways that will not overwhelm them;

- helping children with complex wishes and feelings about contact with both abusers and others who failed to protect them (see Chapter 14);

- helping children and young people to develop a more positive sense of self and to strengthen resilient characteristics (see Chapter 11).

Who keeps the life journey work?

Ryan and Walker (2003) advise:

> 'Without question it belongs to the child. Should he or she, therefore, be allowed to keep it? Of course, but the timing is important…at certain stages some children destroy their life story work if it is in their possession. The child may be overwhelmed by a sense of anger and frustration about what has happened and may direct this at the book. If this happens, valuable photographs and documents may be lost forever (…take photocopies…). In the early stages, therefore, we recommend that you are prudent and make sure that the book is kept in a safe place. At all times the child should have reasonable access to it, but this needs to be supervised.' (p 17)

The child also has the final say about who is allowed to look at the work. Check this periodically as children change their ideas about what is confidential and should be kept from whom and why.

Foster carers

Foster carers often have the most difficult task because they are usually the most close at hand to be asked questions, but may themselves not have enough information. It cannot be said too often that foster carers should be given all the information relevant to each child or young person placed with them, so that they can reinforce everything the social worker is saying to the child.

If the question is about the future and the future is not known, carers should simply explain that no decision has yet been made and what the process of decision-making will be.

If facts about the child's past are not available, carers should gently explain why it is difficult for family members who may be distressed or angry with the local authority for separating them from their children to talk freely to social workers.

If children have been given information by their social worker that is troubling them, it will probably be the foster carers they will choose to talk to. Carers should offer a listening ear and be prepared to ask social workers what they meant, if the child is unclear about some of the language used. If facts are the issue, the social worker should be asked to clarify these.

Often what children and young people will need most of all from their foster family is to be comforted or reassured or to have their spirits lifted.

Adoptive parents

Adoptive parents can sometimes agonise over whether to talk with their children about their past if their histories are particularly traumatic; they may fear that some information would be extremely upsetting, and perhaps the child need never learn about it. What good can it possibly do, for instance, to know that you were born as the result of a violent attack? If the events are buried deep in the child's past, perhaps in infancy, and the child has no memory of them, isn't it better not to let them resurface to cause serious distress, perhaps for life?

All adopters have to make their own difficult decisions about these things. Wanting the best for children is, of course, a good starting point. The most helpful information we have, however, comes from young adopted adults who tell us that it is better for children to be told – and earlier rather than later – in age-appropriate ways, about even very shocking or distressing matters.

It may also be helpful to bear the following in mind.

- Children have a right to information about their origins and lives.

- Many children are able to sense when adults are not being entirely honest with them and find this difficult to deal with.

- Children, when faced with gaps in knowledge about their histories, may invent stories: either unrealistic, wishful fantasies, or horror stories far worse than the truth.

- Children often have disjointed memories from very early years that are disturbing for them and which need untangling.

- If other family members and friends know facts that you want to protect your children from, it is not possible to arrange for everyone to keep secrets forever.

Morrison (2004) addresses some of these problems.

'There are some facts that will always be very difficult to face. Your child may be the result of an incestuous union or of rape. Or possibly…one of the birth parents abused or rejected your child; they may be in prison as a result. Tragic episodes do occur in the lives of some young children, and if this is true of your child it will be necessary to explain what happened, although exactly what you tell and how you tell it will vary as your child grows older and has more understanding of the world. Your language will need to change as time goes on…You may, for example, find it enough with a small child to talk of a birth parent being 'unwell' and (later) be ready to move on to an explanation of 'drugs' or 'alcohol', especially if schools are addressing these issues. You should receive support, advice and, if necessary, access to therapeutic services to help your child survive the effects of this on their development. Helping children learn about limits of behaviour in a caring way…will also equip them to understand when you try to explain that their birth parents did not learn enough about those limits.

'Telling distressing facts may be one issue but you may at a later date be a vital listener. It can be a real shock when a child is finally secure enough to begin to share difficult memories. We might like to think we will find the right words for these situations but logically we know there is no easy answer.

'What you can do is:

- Keep listening.

- Acknowledge your child's courage in beginning to talk.

- Accept whatever feelings are expressed about it.

- Try not to be overwhelmed, or at least don't show it. You will be the best judge of whether your child can accept a hug at such times or needs you to share his or her distress.

- Remember she or he could only share because it felt safe enough – that sense of safety needs to continue.'

(Morrison, 2004, p 42)

A variety of games and exercises are described below. Most can be adapted to the particular needs of children at different operational ages.

Starting

The child may already have a life journey book, photo album or memory box. If so, spend time going through it with the child. This can help you understand how much the child knows and understands about their past, and how you can build on it.

CASE EXAMPLE
SEAN

When Clare first started life journey work with Sean, her adopted son, he showed her his big scrapbook with birthday and Christmas cards stuck in it. For one year, his fourth year, there were no cards or pictures. This was the time when he returned home to his birth family for attempted rehabilitation – which failed. This gave Clare an opportunity to talk with Sean about the inability of his birth mother to care for him and the need to find a permanent family for him.

Understanding others

Some parental failings, like domestic violence or neglect, associated with substance misuse, can be particularly hard for children to accept. You and your child can discuss why a parent needed to resort to blanking out awful situations with alcohol or drugs. List all the positive things he or she remembers about the adult as well as the negative ones. Children will not be able to empathise fully with an adult's situation but may be able to understand that it made them unable to cope with looking after anyone else.

Always make sure the child does not extrapolate from the particular to the general – very few adults resort to drink, drugs or violence when they are finding it hard to cope, and they don't usually die. But children whose parents have died often have only the vaguest idea of what happened.

CASE EXAMPLE
CARRIE AND ROBERT

Carrie and Robert's birth mother died when they were two and five respectively. Four years later when they were living with their adoptive mother, they began talking about life in their birth family: both children remembered the same and some different events, often helping each other fill in the detail. They remembered positive events and other times when they had been frightened. They both wanted to know more about how their birth mother, Meg, had died.

Their adoptive mother, Anna, contacted the local authority. She managed to locate the social worker who had placed the children. The social worker was able to provide information about Meg's fatal drug overdose. She showed them a newspaper article on the incident which also gave details of the church where Meg was buried. Anna, Robert and Carrie talked a lot about drug addiction and how it can badly affect a person's physical and emotional health, leading to an inability to care for the people you love and are responsible for.

Anna and the children eventually wrote down some "Messages for Meg" which wished her peace and rest and took them to the cemetery with a small bunch of flowers.

Helping children develop positive identity and build resilence

Being looked after

Many children who have been looked after carry with them two major questions: 'Who am I?' and 'How did I get here?'

Aspects of the "Who am I" question include:

- personal history;

- ethnicity, sexual orientation, religion, culture and nationality;

- relationships;

- daily occupation and pursuits.

The more often children have to move, the more often they have to accommodate different versions of themselves.

Some children of minority ethnic groups may not always have lived with a family that reflects their ethnicity. Family relationships and contact arrangements may have changed. Different lifestyles in different households and a variety of school routines may add to children and young people losing any sense of a continuous and coherent personal history.

Indeed, looked after children can become highly skilled in being "chameleon-like" – becoming the person they think will help them "fit in" or help them get through a situation. All children who face new situations have a tendency to do this; however, children who have had to do it a number of times may lose sight of the person behind the facade.

Being different

Looked after children and young people often have to contend with being regarded by their peers and by adults as somehow having deserved to be "in care". Many people will not have any understanding of the looked after system. They may make mistaken assumptions about why children and young people become looked after. They are likely not to know the difference between foster care and adoption.

The introduction of designated teachers for looked after children in every school should lead to a better understanding, but this may not spread through the whole school community, or beyond.

Some children will be regarded as being additionally different.

Disabled children

Disabled children generally have to contend with a stereotyping process that sets them apart from their peers.

The cycle of stereotyping can be graphically described as follows.

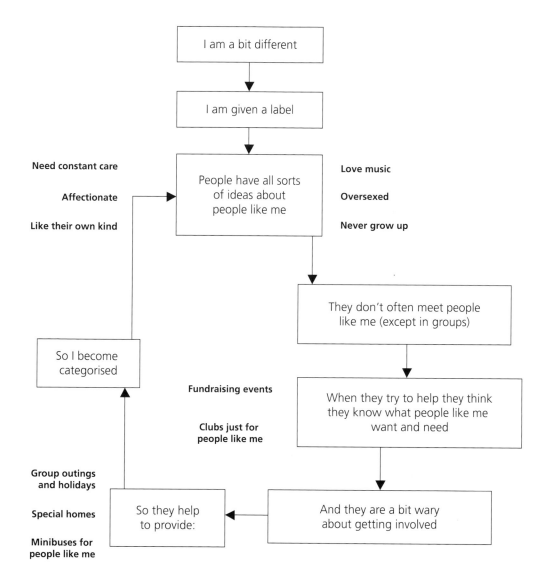

The social model of disability refutes this cycle of stereotyping. It defines disability in terms of the combined effects of impairment and social oppression rather than as a medical condition or human category. It takes into account the role society plays in disabling a person by preventing their full participation in cultural and physical activities.

A disabled young person has described the difference this view makes to him in terms of his identity: 'I have an impairment which means I cannot walk. Society disables me by failing to provide adequate wheelchair access to many buildings.' Older children and young people can feel significantly empowered by the messages this model conveys. It is important, when preparing disabled children and young people for permanence, that they can see themselves as being the best thing that will have happened to their new family rather than being part of some welfare agenda.

Black and minority ethnic children

Black and minority ethnic children and young people are also frequently stereotyped. They are disproportionately represented in the care system in the UK.

White children rarely think about what it means to them to be white; black children tend to highlight issues of their ethnicity when considering aspects of personal identity. Living in a predominantly white, and largely racist, society will have a profound negative impact on black children's sense of self-regard and self-esteem.

Workers and carers undertaking direct work with black and minority ethnic children and children with dual heritage should have a thorough understanding of the cultural, language, faith and community issues that are relevant for each child. Some children will feel more comfortable with a worker who is of the same ethnicity as themselves. Black and minority ethnic children and adults are from diverse, heterogeneous communities; children and young people can feel more able to connect with workers who are from, or who have a good understanding of, their own particular culture.

When a white worker begins direct work with a black child or young person, the worker should explore with the young person what this will mean for them. Some young people will find the issue irrelevant: some will want to talk about how they can engage in work that might raise issues of empowerment and racism with a white worker.

Preparation for permanence with black and minority ethnic children and young people must always include discussion of how their ethnic identity will be promoted and valued in the placement that is being proposed. In practice, workers may encounter situations where an individual black child or child of dual heritage is reluctant to talk about ethnic identity, or is denying his or her ethnic heritage. Practitioners should, of course, start any work with individual children by acknowledging their views and not imposing ideas of how they should feel about themselves. On the other hand, it is not good enough to abandon the work on the basis that 'The child is not ready', or 'It is not currently a problem' for the child. If it is not now, it will be in the future and it may have become compounded by intervening events.

This is a challenging part of work with children. Workers should start with contextual issues. These could include explorations with the child or young person of how their peer groups might include a diversity of individuals (who do/do not reflect their own ethnicity) and what networks their current and future family might belong to. Over time, direct work should gradually address the child's or young person's perceptions of personal ethnicity and how their sense of self might have evolved.

Change and the lack of a coherent history

During the transitions that precede a move to permanence, many children can lose the threads of their own histories. They may not have a personal life narrative that makes sense to them. They probably have not had the advantage of a consistent adult who has been able to hold their memories and who has treasured their life markers for them: first pair of shoes, school reports, books, photographs, etc.

Children who have moved between families need to recover and to have confirmed their remembered and un-remembered past. The list of background information in Chapter 6 can also be taken as a basis for information needed by children and young people moving from one family to another.

Some of their additional questions may be:

- Where was I born? Who was there?

- What day of the week and what time of day was I born?

- What was my birth like? Who visited?

- When did I leave hospital? Who was there and what was I wearing? Did I go in a car?

- Where was my home? With whom? How long did my birth mother care for me?

- When did I lose my first tooth?

- Did I have any brothers or sisters?

- How did I get my name?

- How old were my parents when I was born?

- What did they look like?

- What did they like doing?

- Where did they grow up, go to school? Where did they work?

- What did I look like when I was little?

- When did I learn to walk?

- What were my first words?

- What was my favourite toy?

- What did I like to eat?

- Did I have a pet?

Children need all the recorded and anecdotal information that goes to make up a full picture of "Who I am".

A sense of self, however, does not automatically follow from being given full information about the past, although it is an essential factor. Identity develops from the way a person sees himself or herself and the extent to which this is shared by family, friends and others. Positive identity formation entails compatible, positive regard by oneself and by others of the "Who am I?" aspects listed at the beginning of this chapter. As children grow up, this entails a series of "conflicts" and "resolutions" in order to connect their inner perception of "self" with how others see them. Children joining new families who have had many previous moves may have become used to dealing with a series of "identity conflicts" without having experienced many "resolutions". The impact on their identity formation will be linked to their degree of resilience.

Resilience

'Once children are able to generate meanings that lead to creative and constructive responses to events, they are set on the road to developing resilience.'

(Cairns, 2002, p 144)

Factors that are consistently linked with resilience in children and young people are:

- strong social support networks;

- at least one unconditionally supportive carer;

- a positive school experience;

- a belief that 'I can make a difference';

- an ability to participate in a range of extra-curricular activities;

- the ability to reflect on and consider adversity so that the positive effects can be recognised as well as the negatives;

- the opportunity to experience challenging situations so children can develop and maintain benign coping skills and strategies learnt in recurring situations.

'Resilience comprises a set of qualities that helps a person to withstand many of the negative effects of adversity. A resilient child has more positive outcomes than might be expected given the level of adversity threatening their development. Bearing in mind what has happened to them, a resilient child does better than he or she ought to do. Understanding why some children may make favourable progress in unfavourable circumstances may tell us more about how to help people exposed to potentially damaging situations.'

(Gilligan, 2001, p 5)

Building resilience is key to enabling children to recover from traumatic and adverse experiences; this includes building on self-esteem, self-efficacy, self-reflectivity, social empathy and autonomy (National Assembly for Wales, 2005).

Direct work, together with re-parenting, should aim to help the child develop resilience. Ideas of how this might be undertaken in practice are set out below.

Self-efficacy and self-esteem

Many children who have experienced uncertainty, neglect or abuse, grow up with chronic, global low self-esteem. It has to be a key aim for all adults working with looked after children to help them to feel better about themselves. Self-esteem is a slippery capacity at the best of times, and many children who are moving to a new permanent family have not had the best of times.

It can be very difficult to help raise self-regard and esteem from a low base. We should have optimistic but realistic aims. Our goal is to offer children positive experiences to reframe their ideas of who they are by developing practical, social and relationship skills.

Indicators of high self-esteem include:

- being confident without being overbearing;

- not being devastated by criticism;

- not being overly defensive when questioned;

- being mostly happy with oneself;

- not easily defeated by setbacks and obstacles;

- not needing to put others down;

- being open and assertive in communicating needs;

- being self-reliant and resourceful but not refusing help when needed;

- not being overly worried about failing or looking foolish;

- having the ability to laugh at oneself.

Indicators of low self-esteem may include:

- frequent feelings of jealousy;

- negative talk about oneself;

- frequently criticising others;

- frequent feelings of guilt;

- constantly comparing oneself to others;

- being unable to accept or to give compliments or praise;

- frequently feeling depressed;

- frequently experiencing poor health.

These are not accurate assessment tools, but they can give useful pointers to a child or young person's self-regard. The key aim is to enhance the child's ability to see him or herself as a likeable or even lovable person. This will be a slow process. The first few steps in the journey can be the most difficult. Work with individual children and young people will vary but the following guidance should be relevant to all.

- Offer the child opportunities to use skills he or she already has. It is better to offer many opportunities for small successes rather than the occasional chance of a big achievement.

- Gradually introduce ways of helping the child extend his or her capabilities in general family or school life. Have contingency plans ready to support the child where this proves problematic; children with low self-esteem are likely to feel that they are all-round failures if they do not succeed in a specific task.

- Use play with board games or play-people to practise "winning and losing" (some children will have as much difficulty with succeeding as with not succeeding).

- Model for the child that it is OK both to do things well and to make mistakes. You can even develop a spoken-aloud self-commentary, such as: 'That was a silly thing I did there and I've broken something', or 'Well, I found that quite difficult to try but I am pleased I managed it.'

- Practise social skills with the child in a variety of situations.

- Tell the child what you and others like about him or her and what you and others might find difficult. Help the child to accept being liked and to try to do things differently where this is helpful.

- Humour is a great asset, but beware of making the child feel teased – this is a no-go area for children with low self-esteem.

Self-reflectivity

Our abilities to learn from achievement and adversity are critical to building resilience. Growing into adulthood involves, in this context, moving from a strategy of avoiding the possibility of ever having to repeat an awful experience, to developing ideas of how to do things differently next time.

Children who have had to deal with adversity upon adversity are more likely to have developed avoiding, dissociating strategies. In particular, children who have been traumatised by past events will retain protective behaviours that are highly complex and resistant to change.

Social workers, foster carers and adoptive parents should aim to talk with children about the consequences of their actions and to reflect together on how they might try to do things differently. Again, a range of low-risk opportunities are better than a few high aims for getting things right.

CASE EXAMPLE
KEREM

Kerem, aged 11, was growing up in long-term foster care with Maggie and Tabib. He had been with them for two years and in that time had made and broken a series of friendships with other boys. He very much wanted to be part of a group and/or to have a friend, but the other children in his class found him overbearing and destructive, and did not tolerate him for long. Maggie tried lots of ways to help Kerem with social skills but when ordinary playground difficulties arose, he would resort to controlling behaviours, which left him friendless.

Maggie decided to plan for a big party for Kerem's 12th birthday and to invite nearly the whole class. When discussing this with her support worker, however, she came to realise that the plan would present Kerem with high expectations, which were unlikely to be fulfilled. Instead, she and Tabib arranged an outing to see a film, followed by a birthday tea at home with one other child from the class – Erol and his parents. The birthday was a success and the carers talked with Kerem about why it had gone so well. Erol and Kerem began to visit each other's homes to play computer games and generally hang out. Both sets of parents were able to help Kerem understand what was helpful in the friendship and what was not. This, in turn, helped Kerem to get on better with his peers at school, and slowly to develop his social circle.

Social empathy and autonomy

We can see in the above example that not only was Kerem developing an awareness of how his actions impacted on others, but also why this was so. He was extending his capacity to realise how others feel.

Direct work can assist children and young people to develop social empathy.

Materials could include:

- "feelings" puppets/cards;
- "what if..." scenarios with play-people;
- books/stories.

Methods may include:

- helping the child relate his or her own feelings to those of others;

- putting feelings into words;

- thinking about ways of making/showing "good" and "bad" feelings.

Over time a child will:

- be better able to feel good about himself or herself without needing others' approval;

- be better able to deal with adversity;

- have a greater range of social and coping skills;

- enjoy life more.

Children aged under seven or eight years will still be evolving their abilities to understand ideas about self and others. Their cognitive and language capacities will allow only simple understanding and expressions of self and relationships. That is not to say that these things are not important to very young children, but they need to be expressed in ways that relate directly to the child's experience and, most usefully, through visual images and play.

Young children have short concentration spans and need short and frequent activity periods. They also need to have information repeated to them to reinforce it. Play activities can be varied but repeated within the same session and in subsequent sessions.

CASE EXAMPLE
SAM

Re-read Sam's story in Chapter 6. Here are some additional details.

Sarah, Sam's mother, misused drugs and his father, Luke, was often unable to recognise Sam's physical needs. Sam experienced inconsistent warmth, food and sleep as a baby in their care until he was 15 months old, when he was placed with foster carers on an emergency basis. Following this placement, Sam had a three-month stay with his mother, Sarah, in a hostel, where care was again poor. For the following four months he received adequate care from his grandmother, Betty, and was then placed with new foster carers for nine months. Subsequently, Sam lived with his father, Luke, for 10 months, and from there was placed in his current pre-adoptive placement with foster carers Carole and Kevin.

Sam's failure to thrive in his first year was compounded by his being left with lots of different people when in Sarah and Luke's care. In his first four years of life, Sam had six different primary carers. Despite this, he appeared to develop a positive and healthy attachment to Carole and Kevin. With the exception of his father, all Sam's carers have been white.

Sam's main questions about his identity were:

- Who am I?

- How did I get here?

He also had another question that was worrying him:

- What is going to happen?

His social worker, Elli, who was white, planned three sessions with Sam to help him with his first two questions. She identified five elements to tackle.

- Sam's understanding about who his family is.

- His relationships with his family members and their relationships with each other.

- Sam's feelings about being separated from his family.

- Sam's perceived ethnic identity.

- Sam's understanding of what has happened up until now.

The sessions were to be in a room in the foster carers' house and were to be held once a week on Friday mornings when Sam could stay home from nursery.

First session

Aim: for Elli to introduce herself to Sam and find out how he is generally feeling, and to start establishing Sam's understanding about his current placement and his feelings about being separated from his family and previous carers.

activities:

- Sand and water free play (chosen by Sam) – to help Sam relax and engage with Elli.

- "Feelings" finger puppets – to give Sam the opportunity to talk about his feelings now and previously.

- Black, white and mixed ethnicity play-people – story play about a boy of about Sam's age being looked after by a foster mum and foster dad.

Second session

Aim: to build on the initial work about Sam's feelings about separations and losses and to begin to give him information about his life story.

activities:

- Sand and water free play (chosen by Sam) – to relax Sam and allow him to talk about any thoughts that occur.

- Photographs of mother Sarah, father Luke, grandmother Betty, sister Sophie and Sam as a baby and a two-year-old – talking about memories and what his family liked about being with Sam and the difficulties they struggled with.

- "Feelings" paper plates – drawing happy/sad faces on each plate and exploring how some family situations can be happy and sad at the same time.

Third session

Aim: to build on Sam's understanding of how he is connected to his mother, father, sister and grandmother; to offer further opportunities for Sam to express feelings about separations; and to begin to help Sam to value his white/African-Caribbean identity.

activities:

- Play-dough free play (chosen by Sam) – to offer an open start to the session. Used by Sam to express feelings of frustration and worry about being separated from his father.

- Picture calendar – charting when father Luke will visit.

- Painting – a picture to give Luke at his next visit in two days' time.

- Mirror play – Ellie invited Sam to talk about what/who Sam sees in the mirror. Mirror play with photographs of mother Sarah and father Luke – who do they see in the mirror? Mirror play with photograph of Sophie – who does she see in the mirror? Ellie describes the dual nature of Sam's ethnicity.

This is me

Use a large piece of paper and fold it in half so that it is like a card. Ask the child how they think other people would describe them. Help the child to write these descriptions on the front outside of the card or write for the child if needed.

Then ask the child how they would describe themselves and write these descriptions on the inside of the card. Encourage the child to talk about emotions and traits as well as physical characteristics. Include things they enjoy and things that worry or scare them. End with asking the child what they would like a new family to know about them – the child can choose from the "outside" and "inside" descriptions. If children are able, they could colour or decorate the card. Current carers can be involved in helping the child. This activity will probably need a number of sessions and will vary according to the child's ability to express themselves.

The child's story/a public story

Children need to have an explanation of events in their lives that they can give other people. It needs to be a story that the child feels comfortable with, that is as close to the truth as is possible, but not too complex. Neighbours, friends and children at school will all be curious about where the child has lived before, why they have been adopted and what their history is. Children need to be given confidence about how to answer such questions; they might otherwise fabricate unreal stories and create fantasies around their past.

CASE EXAMPLE
ROBBIE

Robbie was four when he was placed with foster carers Ben and Jane. His father had left the family when he was travelling abroad. Robbie's mother suffered periods of depression and was frequently hospitalised. Robbie and his sister were cared for by different family members and neighbours. When Robbie started school, he told his teacher that his dad was a pilot and 'always flying around' and his mum was a famous actress.

Robbie's social worker helped Robbie talk about what mums and dads do, comparing Ben and Jane's care of him with his experiences with his birth parents. She used role-play to show Robbie that families can be different and that not all mums and dads can look after children safely.

Robbie's story changed over time and he told his next teacher that his first mum and dad found it hard to be a family and that he, Robbie, liked living with Ben and Jane better because they took him to their caravan.

Adoptive parents

Direct work does not stop when children are finally placed with adoptive parents. It is important for the new family to show an active interest in the work that has been done so far; valuing the child's history is a part of valuing the child.

Adoption is a new, exciting start, but it has to remain connected to all the other fragments of the child's life. Continuing to work with children on their never-ending story, to include facts and feelings about their adoption experience, will help to keep the pieces together. In time, more memories from the past may surface and be added to the story; often children wait until they feel safe enough to reveal their deepest emotions or to disclose how they have been hurt.

The aims of and techniques for direct work in permanent placements should be the same as before and during the transition to permanence. But carers must never allow it to become a self-conscious duty or one burden too many; learning to live together, making adjustments, forming attachments, and developing trust can also be called direct work with children.

Ascertaining children's wishes and feelings

'The greatest reassurance we can give children is the feeling that they are understood and accepted – right down to the painful sad bit in the middle.'

(Clare Winnicott, quoted in Kanter, 2004)

Children need to know that they are important – that how they feel and what they want matters. Helping a child to express their feelings can give them the freedom to talk about their wishes for the future.

Listening to children and being sure we have understood what they are saying is crucial to an awareness of how they feel. If we are unsure we must ask the child to say it again or to explain it in a different way. We should repeat back what we think has been said, so that the child can confirm it.

CASE EXAMPLE
TYREECE

Tyreece, aged six, was growing up with his foster carers. They were anxious about how Tyreece was experiencing contact with his mother. Four or five days prior to her visit, Tyreece would start to get tummy aches. They would stop one or two days afterwards. Tyreece, however, would never admit to being worried about the contact.

Tony, Tyreece's social worker, used some "Feelings Faces" cards in guided play with Tyreece. He gave Tyreece headings like "Going to the park" and asked Tyreece to choose the faces that went with them. As the play progressed, Tony introduced headings that related to separations. Tony left the cards with Tyreece's carers so they could continue using them. Tyreece started putting in his own headings and asked Tony to choose the faces. His most telling one was "Saying goodbye to someone". Tony chose the crying face, and then gave Tyreece the same sentence. Tyreece said there wasn't a face that had a tummy on it. Tony used a blank card to draw an empty circle for a tummy; Tyreece asked how to draw a tummy ache. Tony felt he had reached Tyreece's 'painful sad bit in the middle'.

Children who have experienced chaotic or dysfunctional family relationships may have confused, idealised or negative views of families. Preparation for permanence will include helping children and young people to have a more positive and realistic expectation of family life by linking it with the individual child's current or recent experiences of foster care. What aspects of family life did he or she find different, welcome or difficult? When talking to children about a move to a new family, it is important to help them think through their hopes and fears about the future.

Many children will have simple expectations: 'I wanted somebody to look after me and love me and do all that kind of stuff and basically look after me and bring me up properly' (Mandy, aged 11, in Thomas *et al*, 1999, p 38).

activities

Joint storytelling

Joint storytelling can be a way of engaging with children about their history, their feelings and what might happen next. It can be used with children aged three to 12 and can be simple or more detailed according to age.

Ask the child to choose his or her favourite animal and give it a name. Then start telling a story about the animal that echoes the child's own story. After a few sentences ask the child to go on with the story. This will give the child a chance to share their perceptions of past events and how he or she felt about them, which may affect what happens in the future. After the child has added a few sentences you can continue the story again and take the opportunity to concentrate on areas about which the child might feel particularly hesitant or anxious.

Expressing wishes

The BAAF books and resource packs, *Tia's Wishes* (Kahn, 2002) and *Tyler's Wishes* (Kahn, 2003), are useful for ascertaining children's wishes and feelings. The child is given a wand and can make wishes about a range of things: the kind of house they would like to live in; the sorts of activities or hobbies they would like to try; their wishes for 'what happens next'. The stories make it clear that not all wishes come true, so that children are not left thinking that everything is possible.

Expressing feelings – representational work

Children usually enjoy activities such as paper-plate drawing – making happy, sad or angry faces, etc. You can use the paper-plate faces for the child to show how he or she is feeling at the start of a particular session.

Expressing feelings – sensory work

Some children learn early on that expressing their feelings makes them vulnerable to rejection, violence or betrayal. By the time they reach six or seven, keeping their feelings to themselves can have become habitual. Some young people may have stifled their emotions to such an extent that they find it hard to recognise feelings and will have to struggle to talk about them.

You might need to start with activities that encourage young people to use their senses of touch, taste and smell to help them to connect with how their body feels. You can introduce activities that ask them to respond to a variety of smells (lavender/fish and chips/used trainers…). In time, try to encourage the young person to think of some benign activities or situations from their childhood that they may be able to recall through smell or sound. Do not ask the young person to close their eyes during the session, but accept it if it happens spontaneously. Do not attempt to use sensory work to help a young person to re-connect with traumatic events. The purpose is to enable young people to feel and express general feelings. If they are later ready to talk about deeper issues, they will have something to build on.

Using questionnaires

This can be a set of questions or unfinished sentences, which the child can answer, react to and discuss. It is useful for children who are unfamiliar with, or cautious about, sharing feelings. The statements can start off being quite neutral:

> 'My favourite TV programme is…'

> 'My favourite colour is…'

and become more focused:

> 'My favourite person is…'

> 'The person I like least is…'

> 'I get scared when…'

> 'What makes me sad is…'

This activity can help children to express themselves and become more confident in making statements that are negative as well as positive about themselves or other people and situations.

Children who enjoy drawing may like to use a whole page, with the heading 'This is me' or 'These things make me sad' to draw how they see themselves or think others see them.

The questionnaire can be developed into a whole booklet, with the child being encouraged to illustrate it with their own drawings, photos, and stickers.

Helping children think about a new permanent family

Getting ready

Children from the age of three or four prepare for new situations by trying out scenarios in play. Before attending classes at school, children play at schools. Children play at dressing up for social situations they have not yet encountered.

They "practise" in role play or pretend play. Children will find a move to a new permanent family – a significant transition for any child – far easier if they have had an opportunity to play it out beforehand.

This kind of direct work should be guided by the social worker and incorporate lots of opportunities for age-appropriate explanations. The following case example of work with a young girl provides an excellent model for good practice. The model can be adapted for work with boys and with children who are older if the play materials and the commentary are adjusted accordingly.

CASE EXAMPLE
POLLY

Polly was four. The plan was for her to be adopted. Like her siblings before her, she would be placed away from the local area and away from her foster carer. Extensive work about her origins, birth family and key figures in her life had helped her to understand why she was in this foster placement. Polly was able to tell her story using play, language and drawings. However, her social worker, Karen, had not so far broached the subject of adoption or a move to an adoptive family.

Polly at this age had little comprehension about adoption (see Chapter 10). Although she could repeat almost word for word what Karen might say about a forever family, her understanding was less certain. Karen devised a plan to introduce the concept of a placement move and permanence to Polly through play.

Karen already had a good relationship with Polly. She had visited regularly and Polly trusted her. Karen had discovered that Polly loved the colour pink – bright pink preferably, but any pink would do! She also loved teddy bears and little boxes and bags in which interesting items could be hidden or stored. Karen found a small bright pink teddy bear in a high street gift shop. It came in a neat box, and Karen made it comfortable with a little home-made blanket and pillow (both pink, of course!). On her next visit, Karen took Molly Bear with her to visit Polly.

Karen introduced Molly Bear, making sure Polly knew she was a very special teddy. The bear intrigued Polly. It was pink, in a box and was "special", and it had almost the same name as she did. Karen explained that Molly Bear lived in her office (where Polly was convinced Karen also lived) and often came out with her to visit people. Karen shared some of the bear's adventures with Polly, and mentioned that she was finding it very hard to look after Molly Bear properly, but that she loved her very much and was trying her hardest to make her safe and keep her well and happy.

The next visit went along the same lines, but Karen expanded on the challenges she was facing in looking after her special bear. She asked Polly if she knew all the different things that a mummy had to do to look after a little child. They made a list, and Polly connected these tasks to Molly Bear. She asked Karen if she was looking after Molly, keeping her warm, playing with her and making sure she was safe. Polly told Karen that she knew how to look after teddy bears properly, and excitedly ran upstairs to fetch a couple of her well looked after bears so they could tell Karen what a good mummy Polly was.

At the close of the first and second sessions with the teddy bear, Molly was carefully packed up in her box and taken back to the office by Karen.

Next time she came, Karen said almost immediately that she had been trying very hard to look after Molly Bear, but hadn't been able to do all the things she needed to do. She said that she was forgetting to feed her and cuddle her, and that she sometimes left her in the office when she went out on visits. Karen told Polly that she was going to have to find a new mummy for Molly Bear. She said that it wasn't going to be an easy job as it had to be just the right person – someone who would be able to do all the things that you need to do with a special bear so they are safe and happy, and someone who would grow to love Molly Bear just like Karen did.

Polly asked Karen how she was going to find a new mummy. Karen began to explain the process of looking for a new home for Molly Bear. She said she needed to find a very special mummy – perhaps a little girl who loved bears and who knew how to look after them. Polly immediately volunteered! Karen displayed some (planned) hesitation, asking Polly to tell her how she could be sure that Molly Bear would be safe and happy with her. Polly launched herself enthusiastically into this "game". She told Karen that she knew something special about this bear: it could talk. She held Molly Bear up to her mouth and proceeded to talk in a little bear's voice – Molly Bear "said" she loved to visit Polly, and would like her to be her new mummy.

After a "planning meeting" with Polly, Karen agreed to Molly Bear staying for a short time without her. She stayed for two hours (long enough for Karen to do a visit to another family in the area and come back for her).

When Karen called to collect Molly Bear she was sitting with Polly watching television. They had been reading books and singing songs. Polly told Karen that she thought Molly Bear had been a little bit sad because she didn't know where Karen was, but that she had cuddled her and made her feel happy again. Karen and Polly agreed that Karen would visit the following day, and leave Molly Bear to stay overnight with Polly.

The next day, when Karen arrived with Molly, the little bear was a bit upset, according to Polly, who knew just what to do to make her happy. They all went into the sitting room and sat on the sofa and cuddled Molly. They talked about what

Polly needed to do to look after the bear, keeping her safe all night and getting her up and dressed in the morning. Karen asked if she could ring them before bedtime to check everything was OK, and to let Molly Bear know that she, Karen, was OK too. Then Karen left the house.

Later on, just before leaving the office to go home, she rang to check on Molly Bear. Polly answered the phone. She had been waiting for the call and was eager to tell Karen how Molly Bear was doing, and all about their adventures that afternoon. Karen was allowed to speak to Molly Bear too (to the amusement of some of her colleagues listening in).

When Karen came to collect Molly Bear, she said that she needed to find a forever mummy for her. Polly immediately offered. Karen explained that she thought Molly Bear would be very happy if Polly were to be her mummy forever, but that Karen would visit a few times to check everything was fine. Molly "moved in" the next day.

A couple of weeks later (around the time that the adoption panel was considering a match for Polly) Karen again visited. Molly Bear was very much a member of the family by now. She was looking somewhat "lived in", and the box was well used and doubled as a bath, car, wardrobe and hideaway. Karen told Polly that she thought she was doing an excellent job of keeping Molly Bear safe, well and happy and it was time for her to have her forever.

Polly and Karen had a little ceremony with all the teddy bears. A big brown teddy doubled as a judge for the day. The judge asked Molly Bear if she was happy, and if she wanted to write her name in his book. Polly pointedly informed the gathering that the little bear wasn't able to write, but that Polly would help. The judge told Molly Bear that she had a new mummy, a forever mummy called Polly. He gave them a special certificate, and a sticker to wear.

Polly engaged fully with this activity, which was played out over a five-week period. When Karen began to talk to Polly about a forever mummy and daddy for herself, Polly could link the guided play with her own story about why her birth mother couldn't care for her, why she lived with foster carers, and why she too needed a forever mummy to take care of her.

Karen told Polly that she was looking for a very special family for her. Polly said, 'It won't be today, because you want to make sure it's the right family – just like you did with Molly Bear.' Polly explained to Molly Bear that the waiting would be 'scary' but that they would cuddle up and watch TV.

This was by no means an exact role play of the move from foster care to adoption. However, it gave Polly a sense of transitions. She had shown she wanted to have the bear, and knew she could look after it. She realised that Karen needed to make sure she was the right person for the job, and accepted that the bear would initially visit for short periods. Polly had been helped to see that Karen couldn't do what was needed to care for the bear, and so the gentle introduction to adoption began.

We have described the direct work in this case at some length as it illustrates very well how younger children can learn and understand through play with added simple commentary and explanation.

Even children at a very young operational age will have some understanding about what is going on around them, but may not have the vocabulary to express their feelings. This case example demonstrates how a child was able to relate what the social worker was telling her to her own play experience and was able to use play situations to communicate her feelings.

CASE EXAMPLE CONTINUES . . .

When the time came for Polly to begin her own introductions, Molly Bear accompanied her to every outing and meeting with the prospective adopters. She went to their house and was introduced to their family. Then one day, at the end of a visit, quite unexpectedly Polly put Molly Bear to sleep in what was to be her new bedroom. She kissed her goodnight and said she would see her the next day. Polly had moved on.

Foster carers can help by telling stories to younger children about moving from one family to another. BAAF publishes a range of books suitable for children aged up to seven or eight years. These storybooks should travel with the child to his or her new placement. If the prospective adopters have made a "This is Us" album (see Chapter 5), the carers can look at it with the child before and during introductions.

activities

The "Now" calendar

This activity helps to give children a sense of continuity when contemplating a move to a permanent placement.

Draw a simple calendar representing a week on a large piece of paper. Divide each day between morning, afternoon and evening. Talk about what usually happens each morning, afternoon and evening of each day. Help the child to fill in the calendar. Ask which activities or routines are fun, boring or important to the child. Decide together which of these they would like a new family to know about. Include the food and drinks the child likes, TV programmes, indoor and outdoor activities and bedtime routines.

Ask the child if they would like you to use the calendar to tell their new family about them. Encourage the child to talk about some of the things that might have to change in a new household.

Finding out

Use introductory visits to help older children and young people start to think about how the various relationships in their new family might work. Ask the child to find out during the visits (for example) what three things the father in the new adoptive family is looking forward to doing with him or her. Then ask the child also to find out three activities the father would not choose to do with them.

You can vary the questions to include anything the individual child is anxious about – perhaps ways that individual family members show affection or exercise discipline.

Address books

It helps children to stay connected to the present and the past if they can take with them, when they move, the addresses and phone numbers of all the people who matter to them. Creating or filling in an address book can be both fun and reassuring. Attractive illustrated address books can be bought in good children's bookshops.

Staying in touch: talking with children about contact

Planning for permanence away from a child's birth family does not mean that the birth family is removed from the child's thoughts and feelings.

Some adopted people say that a part of themselves is missing because they have had to settle for only second-hand information about their past. Contact – both direct (face-to-face) and indirect (letterbox) – helps many children to maintain a sense of continuity

Finding the right balance between what the child's needs for contact are, and what is achievable and acceptable to all parties, is complex and challenging. The advantages of contact are well documented but in practice establishing meaningful contact is not always easy, not always sustainable and not even appropriate in some cases. For example, if children have been abused by a parent or older sibling, direct contact with other family members can be extremely complicated.

When planning and managing contact arrangements, careful consideration has to be given to the purpose of contact for the individual child. If the purpose is clear and agreed by all parties, then the type and frequency of contact will be easier to determine.

Establishing the purpose of contact

- Will the arrangements for contact fulfil the child's need to remain connected to their birth family?

- Will the contact sustain an already established relationship or will it be a means of building a relationship?

- Is contact being maintained to assist a child with identity issues?

- Is contact to be increased to lead to rehabilitation?

- Does the child need the approval and reassurance of birth family members or previous carers?

- Will contact help to dispel fears and fantasies and help the child to deal with reality?

- Is contact to be decreased to enable the child to move on?

Moving a child on

For some children, foster carers are the first nurturing, safe adults they have lived with. It is imperative to consider not only the role they play in introducing the child to the new family, but also what form of contact they should retain. It is desirable for the foster carer to visit the child in their new home very quickly after placement and again a few weeks later. Children should know that their former carers will come to see them, and that when the carers leave they will stay in the adoptive home with their new family.

CASE EXAMPLE
RHIAN AND JACK

Rhian, aged three, and Jack, aged four, were taken back to see their foster carers a month after they were placed for adoption. They had been with these foster carers for the preceding 18 months. The children immediately made themselves at home again and when the time came to leave they did not want to go. Two hours later, on their way home, the children and the adoptive mother were distraught and drained, despite the best efforts of the foster carer.

The adopters were inclined to stop any further contact with the foster carers, given that the visit had been so difficult. They talked with their adoption support services adviser who knew both children. She visited twice and each time played a game with the children using play-people who were moving house. The play-children moved with all their clothes and toys to a new family they loved, but they had to leave behind someone they loved as well. They learned that people can still love them even if they are not living with them.

A month later the foster carer visited the adoptive home and had a lovely afternoon in the company of Rhian, Jack and their parents. The visits continued happily for two years.

For children beyond infancy, contact with family members may be less than straightforward because by this stage children are likely to have formed disordered or insecure attachments to birth family members.

CASE EXAMPLE
AMY

Amy was asked how she would feel about continuing to see her birth father, who was supporting her adoption. She described her feelings as sick-sad, happy-sad and hurting-my-heart sad, but she was adamant that she would still like to see him.

activities

Photographs and life journey books

A good place to start is the child's life journey book, together with any photographs of the people with whom contact is being considered. Start with questions such as 'Who is the baby in this picture?' and 'Can you tell me about this one?'

Gradually move towards encouraging the child to recall memories of being with that person. Use simple reflecting-back questions, to help them put into words some of the feelings they are getting in touch with. Go slowly and do not be afraid to leave the subject if the child wants to, but enable him or her to return to it later if possible. Repeat the exercise, or a version of it, in subsequent sessions, and note any consistencies or variations.

Do not discount any feelings if they are apparently contradicted later; children may have valid feelings that seem incompatible but are nevertheless strongly held by them at one and the same time.

My best holiday

This is an "imagination" game – good for using on car journeys or during a quiet time with the child.

Ask the child to think of somewhere he or she would like to go for a holiday.
Then ask:

- Who would the child like to take (anyone from the past or present/alive or deceased/still in touch or not)?

- Where would they all be sleeping (a tent, caravan, hotel)?

- How many rooms/tents/caravans would there be?

- How many people would be in each room/tent, etc?

- Who would they put together in each room?

- Is there anyone on the list who would not be able to come? How does the child feel about this?

- Not everyone is going to fit into the holiday home – some people will have to be left behind. Who would that be?

- Who would definitely come on the holiday? Why?

This game can establish which people the child has the strongest attachments to – both in the past and present – and therefore who it may be hardest for them to separate from when they move.

Piles of love

Another activity to ascertain children's feelings about people they may or may not have contact with is the Piles of Love game. This is especially suitable for children who have few language skills. It helps explore relationships and generates discussion about possible future contact with significant people in the child's life.

Use a large piece of flipchart paper, draw circles and write the names of the main people in the child's life in each circle (these should be people from the past and present, people they like and don't like). Use photographs if the child will find it helpful.

Give the child a pile of beads, buttons, or raisins (beware of small objects with very young children). Explain that this is their pile of love and invite the child to share it among the people in the circles according to how much love they have for them. Each circle may get a pile of love – but perhaps they will be different sizes. Give the child time to change their mind and move the beads around. Then talk about who has the largest pile, the next largest, who may have none.

You can photograph the work produced, showing graphically how the child experiences these relationships. This game can be played prior to placement, during introductions and/or following the move. As with all activities, it should be repeated at intervals to see if the child's perceptions have changed.

Workbooks

Books produced by BAAF such as *Tia's Wishes*, *Nutmeg gets a Letter* and *What is Contact?* are useful in helping children deal with contact and involving them in contact plans for their future (see Bibliography). Some of the most effective work can be done if social workers use these tools as a guide and personalise the accompanying discussion to reflect the particular child's situation.

Children will often think of questions between sessions. Remind younger children that they can ask their foster carers to remember the questions for the next session. Older children can be encouraged to write down questions as they think of them, so they do not get forgotten.

CASE EXAMPLE
AMY

Amy wanted face-to-face contact with her father following placement for adoption and this was agreed. During the week prior to the first contact visit, Amy wanted to know:

- *Who else will be there?*

- *Will my father know where I live?*

- *Can I hug him?*

- *What will I call him?*

- *What if I want to go after five minutes?*

- *What if he gives me the sweets that make me go funny? (A reference to a sweet that her adoptive mother felt affected her behaviour.)*

- *What if he starts shouting?*

Amy's social worker and adoptive parents were able to reassure her and answer her questions. By involving her birth father in the discussion, many of his fears were allayed as well.

Changing the plan

In some cases, the plan to reunite a child with their birth family is changed over time to permanent placement outside the birth family. Current contact arrangements will reflect the original plan. It is important to talk with the child not only about new plans for the future, but also about any changes that are indicated for contact arrangements. Children should be assured that their views matter and that any changes to contact arrangements will be discussed with them before placement.

CASE EXAMPLE
NATHAN

Nathan was angry and upset with his adoptive family. He told them that while he had been in foster care he had spoken to his mother every week on the telephone. It had stopped when he moved. It was their fault and he didn't like them.

This situation could have been prevented if his social worker had involved Nathan and prepared him for the change. Nathan did not know that contact was stopped because his birth mother did not support the placement. He also didn't know that his birth mother had been sending a letter every six months and receiving one back from the adopters.

All of these arrangements should have been included in the social worker's preparation work with Nathan and shared by his adoptive parents so that they could better help Nathan cope with being upset.

Contact arrangements between siblings

Relationships between siblings are often the longest in our lives. Siblings can hold reciprocal insights from childhood which adults do not share. These are relationships to be nurtured unless, in a specific case, this is not consistent with a child's welfare needs.

A frequent reason for the separation of siblings is that they became looked after at different times (Kosonen, 1996). Sometimes younger siblings are not even born when older ones start being looked after.

CASE EXAMPLE
WAYNE AND NOEL

Wayne and Noel were placed separately in long-term foster homes, having become looked after at different times. The reason for this was not explained to the boys and both blamed the other for their entry into the care system. It was understood that their relationship had been, and remained, poor. This issue was belatedly addressed in (separate) direct work with each young person. The social worker gradually moved towards joint direct work with them. This allowed contact in a structured environment and facilitated a gradual improvement in their relationship.

This case illustrates the importance of explaining to children why they are not living with a brother or sister. We know that in general siblings do better if they can remain together but there may be valid reasons, in some cases, for separating sibling groups.

The three reasons most frequently given by children about why they want to be with a brother or sister are:

- a strong emotional bond;

- concern for the safety of a sibling;

- the child has looked after a younger sibling.

What children want and what will meet their needs do not always match. Direct work can help a child gain some insight into their own wishes and feelings about staying in touch with siblings.

CASE EXAMPLE
GARETH

Gareth, aged seven, was living happily with his adoptive family. However, he very much wanted to see his birth half-brother Morgan who was then aged 16 and was in secure accommodation. His social worker, Rob, spent some time with Gareth re-visiting his life path, including the times he had lived with Morgan, and the ways in which Gareth's life had changed since his adoption.

In one session, Rob asked Gareth to think of three things he would enjoy about seeing Morgan and three things he would not enjoy. Gareth thought about this a lot and, after some discussion and pencilling things in and rubbing them out, he wrote in pen:

LIKE

He looked after me

He makes me laugh

We both write with our left hand

DON'T LIKE

He wants me back in Aberystwyth

He hit me

He hates social workers

Rob invited Gareth to go back to this list periodically and in the next few weeks Gareth's "Don't like" list became twice the length of his "Like" list. Gareth and Rob came to an agreement that direct contact with Morgan at this time was not a good idea. Gareth decided that he wanted to send Morgan a card on his birthday and at Christmas. Gareth, his adoptive parents and the social worker talked about it and agreed that it would be a good idea. Gareth became more settled. He and his parents arranged that the social worker would let them know Morgan's new address when he moved.

It is important to continue to talk with children about arrangements that are in place for both direct and indirect contact. Children's needs change as they grow up, and contact arrangements should be reviewed periodically. It is helpful for adopted children to have a named person, perhaps the adoption support services adviser in the local authority, with whom they could discuss these and other issues.

Letterbox contact

The following suggestions have been made by adopted children and young people (and their parents) if letters and cards rather than face-to-face meetings are the contact arrangements:

- Children of all ages can contribute to letters and cards to mark birthdays, special days and holidays.

- Children can decide what and who should be photographed, and choose which photos to send to whom.

- Drawings and paintings by children for specific people are usually much appreciated. One birth mother turned her daughter's drawings into laminated placemats and proudly displayed them.

- Video tapes, particularly between siblings, can be a way to develop a skill and to make communication fun.

- Audio cassettes can work well for families who are not used to writing letters.

- Paint-prints or outline drawings of feet and hands can be contributed by children who do not communicate with words.

- Copies of most recent school reports and certificates of achievement are a good way to keep up with a child's progress.

- Birth families can send up-to-date material for life journey books.

- Email and texting are fast becoming the most common way to communicate, but they are more difficult to monitor.

- Absent people can be kept in mind – two sisters hold hands for a minute every year on their birth mother's birthday.

Helping children with separations and losses

Saying goodbye to people who have been important to us is painful. Partings for children are additionally distressing when they are separating from their source of security, even if that security was overshadowed by neglect and abuse.

Neimeyer (2001) suggests that when we lose a person we also lose the meaning that the person has had for us. So if a person has given comfort, we lose not only that person, but we are also bereft of comfort, not having the capacity in grief to accept comfort from anyone else.

Some looked after children are clear that they will not be reunited with relatives or carers. Others are uncertain about whether the separation will be permanent. Direct work can help children to understand and accept permanent separations.

CASE EXAMPLE
CARYS AND MAIR

Carys and Mair's adoptive mother, Olwen, approached the adoption support service. Her girls were aged eight and six. They had been placed with her 18 months previously and the adoption order had been made six months ago. Olwen was anxious about her children's deteriorating behaviour, which she said was becoming far more difficult to handle.

Robert, the support worker, undertook a series of direct work sessions with Carys and Mair. They had been brought up by their grandmother and when she became ill and frail they were placed in foster care until they were adopted. Robert concentrated on their feelings about being separated from their grandmother, who died while they were in foster care.

It transpired that they had been told of their grandmother's death some time after the event. They did not know about her funeral. Robert was able to work with them and their adoptive mother to help them grieve for their grandmother. This work addressed their worries that Olwen too might die. The children also needed to understand that their grandma was gone forever and they would not be seeing her again. Olwen took her girls to visit their grandma's grave, and she and Robert helped them to make a book of memories including pictures and stories of their growing up with their grandma.

Children's reactions to separation and loss

Young children can feel completely bewildered and emotionally lost if separated from the adults who have been responsible for their care. Their grief is compounded if they are not helped to understand the context and reasons for the separation. Children will use fantasy to fill in gaps in their information and understanding, and can reach a stage where they are unclear about what is real and what is not. In order to cope with everyday living, they elaborate their own ideas about what has happened and what will happen in the future.

Children who are operating at a stage of magical thinking (see Chapter 4) can believe both that it was their fault that they have been separated (bad behaviour/too demanding) and that if they wish hard enough they will be reunited. Children can become angry if anyone tries to change their views. They can ricochet between being over-dependent on carers and rejecting them. They can experience profound distress and despair at one time and present sullen, withdrawn behaviours at another.

If this situation is not resolved, children may become listless and uncommunicative. They may abandon skills and abilities they have most recently acquired and revert to an earlier, more understandable stage of their lives.

Children of all ages can develop acute anxiety that current carers will also disappear without warning; they will develop strategies for keeping carers in sight and limiting the times they are separated from them. Going to school, going to bed, staying home while carers go to work or go shopping can all be worrying situations for them.

CASE EXAMPLE
SARAH

Sarah, aged eight, lived with her Auntie Vera. Vera had been named a testamentary guardian by Sarah's mother, a single parent, who died of cancer when Sarah was five. Sarah was consumed with worry that her Auntie Vera would also get ill and die. She felt she had to look after her constantly to make her remain well and healthy. Sarah's class was to go on a weekend residential visit to a holiday centre. Sarah did not want to go and had tantrums when Vera tried to persuade her. Sarah was certain that it was not safe to leave her auntie for a whole weekend.

Vera's solution was to go away herself that weekend to a "health spa" where she could exercise (lightly), swim (sit in the jacuzzi) and have nice massages and nail manicures. Sarah was eventually reassured that Auntie Vera would be in good hands and she also did not want to deprive her auntie of a treat. Sarah became persuaded that she could safely join her class on the weekend trip.

Older children can better understand explanations about separations from parents and carers. They may have lots of questions while trying to fit memories and earlier understandings into a more mature comprehension. They are able to express thoughts and feelings in words and so can take advantage of more in-depth direct work. Older children can be more accepting – indeed more matter of fact – about some issues of loss.

> ## CASE EXAMPLE
> ## JOHN AND LUCY
>
> *Lucy rushed into the kitchen where her mother was cooking supper. 'Mum, John's flushed Guppy (pet goldfish) down the loo!' Their mother, calling John, asked him why, when he had found Guppy floating and dead in his bowl, he hadn't come to her. 'Well, Mum, I knew if I told you, you'd want to talk about it and I wanted to watch Blue Peter...'*

Adolescents tend to grieve in much the same way as adults do, but as they are still in the process of leaving their childhood years, they can experience intense emotional "ups and downs". Most young people have times when they are withdrawn, depressed or have mood swings. If they are additionally coping with the loss of parents, siblings or other important people in their lives, these periods can intensify. They may prefer to seek comfort from friends rather than parents or carers. They will still need to know, however, that parents and carers are available for emotional support. Young people can experience extreme sadness. They sometimes have to battle with depression; they might use alcohol or drugs or can embark on risk-taking behaviours. They need the adults in their lives to work together to establish rules and boundaries to keep them safe. Young people can benefit from active pursuits that will boost health and so reduce the risk of depression and addiction. They should also be helped to maintain a healthy diet, which otherwise might be abandoned in favour of sugary or fatty foods or under-eating.

Some young people can gain comfort and insights from creative writing and reading, making and listening to music, and seeing films or plays. Time spent alone and (although it might be inexplicable to parents and carers) long hours on the phone, even with friends they have only just left, can really help.

For many children, separations will involve far more complicated feelings than a simple yearning to be reunited. Children who have been abused or neglected may have mixed-up feelings of love, fear, anxiety, responsibility, or sympathy for a parental abuser or a parent who failed to nurture and protect them. New families will be a more challenging prospect than just a "new chapter" in these children's lives.

We should recognise that children will miss not only birth family members but also others they have been close to – friends, teachers and foster carers.

> ## CASE EXAMPLE
> ## ABASI AND MAALIC
>
> *Abasi and Maalic, brothers aged seven and nine, were moved against their wishes from an out-of-county placement where they had been for 18 months, so that their own local authority could better support the placement, and they could have contact more easily with their father who had poor mental health. They had been extremely well cared for by their foster carers Ephrem and Helina and very much wanted to stay; Ephrem and Helina also wanted the boys to stay with them.*
>
> *When Abasi and Maalic were moved, they were angry and upset. Their new foster carers were a white couple living in rural Wales who had little understanding of Abasi and Maalic's faith needs and dietary preferences. The boys still saw little of*

their father, who was in hospital, and they hugely missed their previous foster carers and friends.

Their social worker and new foster carers were unable to empathise with the boys' feelings, tending to concentrate on their father's and extended family members' potential involvement with them. The boys were clear that the most important people in their lives were the foster carers from whom they had been separated against their wishes, and they did their best to sabotage their new placement.

Children of all ages who are grieving for lost adults or other children can present a range of behaviours, which may include:

- physical pains such as stomach aches or headaches;

- difficulty in sleeping, or over-sleeping, or having bad dreams;

- eating too much or too little;

- being destructive;

- angry outbursts;

- repetitive behaviours or play;

- short concentration spans, with consequences for schoolwork;

- switching off, not taking in what is happening;

- self-blame and self-punishment;

- idealising the absent person;

- mood swings;

- excessive separation anxiety;

- running away;

- avoiding company, including school;

- stealing or lying without any apparent purpose.

Direct work addressing separations should be combined with a focused parenting strategy for carers/adopters to help with practical daily living and with encouraging more benign coping behaviours.

activities

Life path (see Chapter 16)

Ecomaps (see Chapter 16)

Life Journey work (see Chapter 10)

Questionnaires (see Chapter 12)

Feelings pictures

Ask the child to draw a picture of himself or herself and the things they like best or enjoy, and which make them happy. See if they can give the picture a title or caption.

See then if the child can do the same for things that they don't like and which make them unhappy. This can help the child identify times when they were separated from people they loved and when they felt sad or angry.

Referring back to the "happy" pictures can encourage the child to see that feelings can change.

Working with sibling groups

Siblings who are to be placed together

Some looked after siblings will always have lived together. Some will have been separated and recently reunited in a placement, while others will have lived apart for some time or may never have lived together. Sibling groups moving to a shared placement may have other brothers or sisters placed elsewhere, and some may have full or half-siblings remaining at home. Sometimes children will feel close to siblings they have been separated from, but in other cases they may hardly know them; indeed, children may not know of the existence of brothers or sisters elsewhere.

Whatever their particular history, the aim of direct work with siblings will be to help them understand their sibling relationships better and to maximise the potential of the planned placement for each child. This will mean, depending on the needs of each child and group, a mix of individual work and joint work.

Siblings who are to be placed separately

Relationships with siblings might be one of the few constant factors in the lives of "looked after" children. Thus, any decision to separate them permanently must be taken with great care. If it is assessed that separation is in the children's best interests, then opportunities and means for the children to maintain some form of meaningful contact must be seriously considered.

Children who are to be separated from their siblings must be given age-appropriate but full explanations for this, together with ample opportunities to explore and express their feelings.

Any child being permanently separated from one or more siblings should be clear about the connection, the nature of the relationship and the reasons why it is deemed best for them not to be placed together. This means children will first of all need to have a clear picture of who all the people in their family are and how they are related.

Aims and practice in direct work with sibling groups

The nature of children's relationships evolves in the context of their shared and individual experiences. One child may have had to take on a caring or protective role, several children may have had to compete for adults' attention, one may have been the favoured or the rejected child. An abused child may also have been the "special" child, setting them apart from their siblings.

All the aims of direct work described in Chapter 4 are relevant to sibling groups and to individual children within each group. There may also be some additional aims such as:

- aligning the children's memories and perceptions;

- ascertaining how the wishes and feelings of each child might impact on future plans;

- establishing positive and empathetic ways of relating and being together;

- helping the children understand how they are connected to each other and to absent family members;

- sharing ideas of what living together in the proposed permanent placement might be like.

Many of the activities described elsewhere in this guide will be suitable for both individual and shared work. You will need to sharpen your observational skills to learn how siblings' perceptions and expectations might agree or differ, and to identify patterns of sibling behaviour.

It is a good idea to allow an extended period of free play during the initial joint sessions to help you observe interactions. Make sure you intervene if children need an adult to sort out differences: not too early in case you lose vital information, and not too late in case they then don't feel safe in your charge. Social workers, foster carers and, where applicable, adoptive parents will need to work closely together to check out their impressions of the developing situation and to maintain compatible strategies.

activities

A family tree

Young children can be shown a family tree – this could be a drawing of a real tree, perhaps an apple tree as pictured below. You can draw a line down the middle from the top to the base of the tree, so that the branches on the left hand side have apples with the names of birth family members and the right hand side depicts members of the new family.

The child will be a moveable apple, going from left to right – you can talk about all the family connections and the child can explore his or her feelings about each person and about moving. The child can help to draw the family tree and can choose what kind of tree it should be.

Older children also like this exercise but many may prefer to be involved in drawing a genogram. These can be useful for sibling groups with complicated family relationships.

CASE EXAMPLE
GEMMA AND SOPHIE

Gemma is seven, Sophie is five and they are full sisters. Gemma and Sophie have two older half-brothers Jack (10) and Tom (eight) and a younger half-brother Nathan (two).

Their mother, Jane, met Alan when she was 16 and their baby, Jack, was born when she was 17. The three of them lived with Alan's parents for a year. When Jane was pregnant with Tom, she left Alan and went to live in a women's refuge with Jack. Tom was born while Jane was still in the refuge, but they were re-housed soon after to a small flat near Jane's sister.

Jane met Bob and became pregnant with Gemma when Tom was a year old. After Gemma's birth, Jane, Bob and the three children moved to live near Jane's mother. When Gemma was nearly two years old Jane became pregnant again. Sophie was born shortly after Bob was sent to prison. Jane was unable to manage the children on her own and asked for Jack and Tom to be accommodated. They were placed in a foster home and remained there for almost a year. Gemma was cared for by Jane's mother but went back to Jane when Sophie was six months old.

When the boys returned home, Jane became depressed and began drinking quite heavily. Social services were involved again when neighbours reported that the children were left on their own while Jane went out drinking.

An interim care order was granted and Tom and Jack were accommodated in a second foster home. They were four and six years old; Gemma and Sophie were three and one. Over the next few months, the girls were often looked after by Jane's mum.

Jane met Steve and they moved back to the area where Jane had first lived, away from Jane's mother. Tom and Jack remained in care.

A different local authority became involved, and although the girls were placed on the Child Protection Register, there was no social work contact with the family for several months. Gemma began arriving at school with unexplained bruising, and staff at Sophie's nursery complained about her poor attendance.

Nathan was born when Gemma was five and Sophie two. Police were called one evening and an Emergency Protection Order was made in respect of Gemma and Sophie. Nathan was looked after by Steve's parents.

Gemma and Sophie were placed with foster carers Mr and Mrs S on a short-term basis. They were moved after two months and placed with Mr and Mrs D. The girls' flow chart is set out below.

Gemma's flow chart

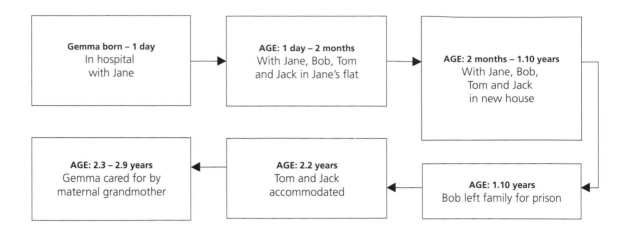

Gemma and Sophie's flowchart

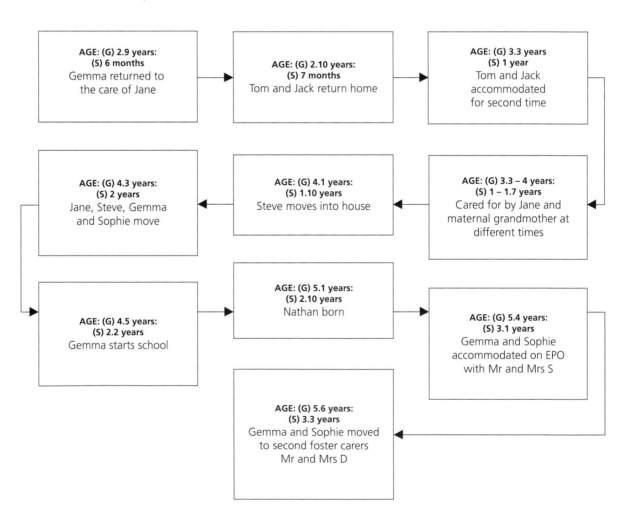

Circles

It may be easier to work with overlapping family circles. Using clear, coloured plastic sheets can give a simplified illustration of family connections. Alternatively, children might like to colour the circles in with crayons to denote the different family groups.

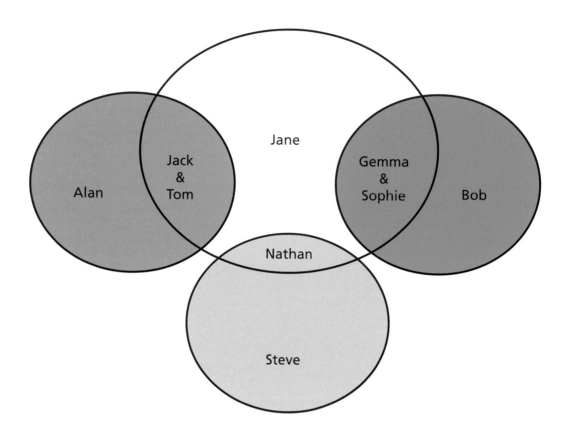

The use of circles can also help to reinforce the idea that, although separated, the links between the siblings will always be there.

Life pathways

The next stage in the work should be to consider the shared or divergent history of the children – the "when" and "why" they came to be looked after together or in different families. Using a life pathway can provide a visual picture of the different directions children's lives have taken (see also Chapter 10).

With young children this can be done as a floor exercise. The path can be made to look like stepping stones, paving stones or even footprints. Footprints could be drawn in increasing sizes to give the impression of the growing child at each step.

Each piece of the path depicts a stage in the child's life. The worker or the child can draw or write on each piece a description of the sibling relationships at the time. If siblings are placed separately, they should be able to see how their pathways have diverged.

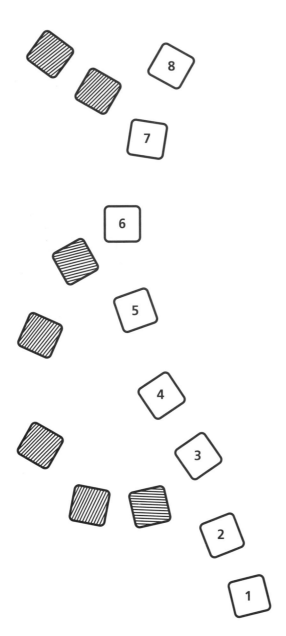

1 – **Gemma born**
   Gemma living with Jane, Bob, Tom and Jack

2 – **Gemma 1.1 years**
   Bob leaves family

3 – **Gemma 2.2 years**
   Tom and Jack live with foster carers

Tom and Jack's path

4 – **Gemma 2.3 years**
   Gemma living with grandmother.
   Sophie born

5 – **Gemma 2.9 years, Sophie 0.6 years**
   Gemma living with Jane and Sophie

6 – **Gemma 2.10 years, Sophie 0.7 years**
   Jack and Tom come home to live
   with Jane, Gemma and Sophie

7 – **Gemma 3.3 years, Sophie 1.0 years**
   Tom and Jack go to live with foster carers

8 – **Gemma 3.10 years, Sophie 1.7 years**
   Gemma and Sophie living with Jane
   or grandmother

Collages

Older siblings can create a wall collage, and add new steps to the path as their worker talks them through the periods they have spent together or apart. To make the exercise more visual photographs or drawings can be added to parts of the path, showing the children at different ages. Try to find photographs of siblings when they were living together. Drawing them would be a good second best.

It will be important not to "fudge" any answers to questions the children might have about separation from their siblings. For instance, telling Gemma and Sophie that their brothers were placed in foster care because their mother, Jane, could not keep them safe would be more honest than saying she had too many children to look after.

The final stage in the work will be to reassure children that their siblings will be safe and cared for, and that they will remain part of their lives – even at a distance.

Drawing an ecomap can demonstrate in a visual way that a link will be retained.

Gemma and Sophie's ecomap

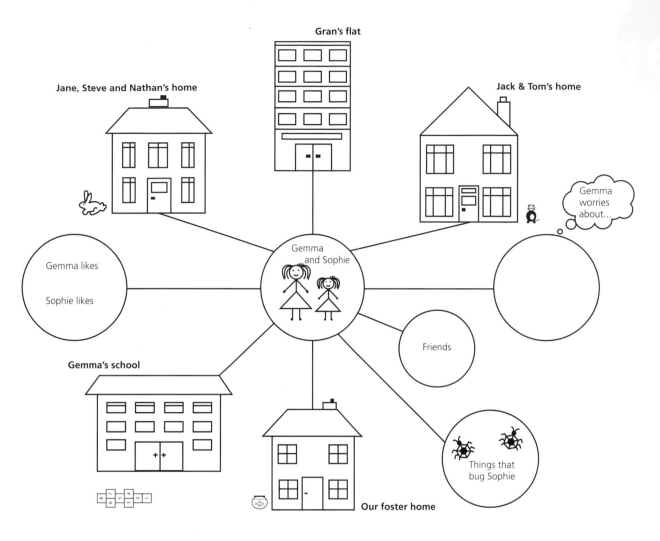

Children will need to know what, if any, future contact arrangements there are to be with their siblings, how these arrangements will be managed and what will be expected of them. They also have to be made aware that sometimes these arrangements can fail to materialise – and why this might happen, and with whom they can talk about it.

Introductions and moves to a new family

Everything we know from professional experience and research tells us that every move matters for children. The experience of too many looked after children is that their move from home is sudden and unplanned. Many children have little advance warning and have not been involved in the decision, which reinforces their anxiety about any future moves.

Planned moves are less harmful: they enable the child to be prepared and to make more sense of what is happening. Even looking at a "This is Us" album with their social worker on the way to a placement has made moving a little less troubling for many children.

When children or young people are going to move to a new permanent family, the plan should always be shared with them in age-appropriate ways, and they should be included in making the arrangements.

If moves are not planned, are not explained to children or are not managed properly, children can find them considerably more difficult and frightening.

CASE EXAMPLE
COLIN

Colin was 14 when he was removed from home. He had been beaten regularly for years by his stepfather and the latest assault had brought Colin to the attention of social services. Colin described the move.

> *'I was in a car. I was being taken away from home. I knew I was going to someone called Carol and Alan. I had no idea where. I had no idea who they were. My heart was thumping. I could feel the blood pounding in my head. I was worried about whether we'd get there before I was sick.'*

Planning introductions

If the child is being adopted, the arrangements will usually begin with a meeting to plan introductions. The main purpose of a planning meeting is to try and ensure that there is a shared understanding about how new relationships must be allowed to develop slowly. These meetings are not always comfortable or straightforward. Often the various parties have different feelings and expectations, and these all have to be considered in order to negotiate an acceptable and workable plan.

The child's social worker, the foster carers' supervisor and the worker for the new family must together ensure that everyone supports the introduction plan. Children can experience feelings associated with moves long before they are able to understand the detail. They can detect any ambiguity workers may have about what is being proposed. Children will have their own mixed feelings about change, and they will manage better if they are not also having to contend with uncertain adults.

Each step of the planned introductions should be monitored, with at least one more meeting of the adults involved before the final move. Arrangements should not be regarded as finite and should be changed by agreement if necessary.

Good supervision from line managers can help significantly.

Moves for the pre-verbal child

It is misguided to assume that placements of very young children are never complicated. In many cases children will be securely attached to the foster carers from whom they are being moved. It is essential that the plan is based on a smooth transfer of the child's connection from his or her foster carer(s) to the new parent(s). This means, ideally, harmonious progress based on the shared understanding of the child's needs. This is not always easily achieved.

The importance of a pre-adoptive foster placement is that it provides an invaluable basis for life with the permanent family. The child may have had very little experience of consistency, continuity and "normal" family life prior to being in foster care. There is a delicate balance between helping the child to feel settled and part of one family and helping him or her to feel ready to become a full member of another family.

Pre-verbal young children will rely largely on the non-verbal signals they get from the adults around them.

CASE EXAMPLE
CHANTELLE

Chantelle's foster carers had looked after her for a year, from the age of six months, when adopters were introduced. On the first visit by the adopters to the foster home, the male foster carer held Chantelle on his lap for the entire visit. He said that she was shy and needed to feel safe. The same thing happened on the second visit. On the third visit when the adopter tried to encourage Chantelle to play, she clung to the male carer and cried. The adopters rang their support worker and said they couldn't proceed with the introductions 'because it would break Chantelle and her carers' hearts'.

Foster carers can feel protective towards the child if inexperienced prospective parents struggle with simple parenting tasks or, conversely, they can feel jealous as the new family and the child begin to bond. Prospective parents may not necessarily agree with the foster carers' parenting methods and can feel frustrated at having to wait until they can parent on their own.

Generally, the younger the child, the shorter and more intensive is the introduction. The introductory period, even if quite brief, should be planned in detail enabling such tasks as feeding, dressing, playing, bathing and putting the child to bed to be gradually taken over by the new parents. First meetings should take place in the foster home with the foster carers present. It is unlikely, although not unheard of, that a child will immediately interact with the visitors, and prospective parents should be aware of this.

It is important that carers encourage pre-verbal children to connect with new parents and praise them for doing so. Prospective families can bring something special on their first visit (perhaps a cuddly toy or an audio cassette with nursery rhymes), which they can leave with the child. They can introduce more toys later, but should agree with the child to look after some of them in the new home, so that the child will find familiar objects there.

When children visit their new family and eventually stay overnight, they should be encouraged to leave some toys or other things from the foster carers' home to help with continuity.

During introductions in the foster home, the new parents' faces should become the last faces seen by children at night, and the first faces seen on awaking in the morning. This helps children to encompass change while in familiar surroundings and enables prospective carers to learn the child's routines. New parents should also incorporate familiar sensory experiences for the pre-verbal child during and following a move. Singing the same lullaby, using the same baby powder or the same teat on the feeding bottle can make infants and toddlers feel safe.

CASE EXAMPLE
JULIAN

Julian had lived with David and Colin from the age of one and was two-and-a-half when the prospective adoptive parents were introduced.

His attachment to David and Colin was very strong and they were worried about how Julian would make sense of this move. The adopters visited daily for a week but Julian continued to look to David and Colin for his care and comfort. David decided to invite the adopters to stay for a weekend. The adopters accepted and on the first night they got up for Julian when he woke at 2.00am. They picked him up from his cot when he woke in the morning and during the weekend they undertook most of his care. David and Colin found lots of excuses to be busy or to pop out. On Sunday evening Julian pulled the adoptive mum's arm when it was time for his bath.

Once a rapport has been established, it is sensible to begin to move the focus to the new family environment. It is usual for a young child to have not more than one or two overnight stays at the new home – it is confusing for small children to go repeatedly back and forth. The change of environment becomes even more disorientating if there is a significant amount of tiring travelling to unfamiliar surroundings.

It is important that new parents (with a social worker but never a social worker on their own) collect the child from the foster home for the final move. All the child's belongings should go with them as well as any goodbye presents from the foster carers and other people.

The musical mobile that hung over the child's bed in the foster home should go above the cot in the child's new bedroom. Similarly, bedtime and bathtime items should move with the child so that daily tactile, auditory and visual experiences can continue. New parents should stick closely to the child's routine following the move and only begin to vary it to suit their own circumstances when the child is more settled. It is widely acknowledged that children can regress to earlier behaviour following a move. This is usually a protective and temporary change. If parenting styles can be adjusted to accommodate a child's needs, it will gradually help them to feel more secure.

Moves for the verbal child

Understanding

Older children will have some understanding of the idea of moving to a new family and, if relevant, the differences between foster care and adoption. Older children can also comprehend that the process will include an opportunity to meet the family before a final decision is made. They should be helped to know that their views are important and will be listened to, but that they are not totally responsible for making decisions.

The reasons for the move should be explained clearly to children. It is essential for children to receive the same information (using the same vocabulary) from all the important adults in their life. Every explanation will probably need to be repeated. Social workers and foster carers should tell the child about their new family, household and environment. Just as potential parents want to know as much as possible about their new child, so children will want to know as much as possible about their new family.

Messages

The most important message that a child needs to have from all parties is permission to form attachments to new parents. Older children may feel particularly anxious about this if they are afraid of hurting their present carers or birth family members.

Foster carers must be given the opportunity to talk through their feelings about letting the child go. Helping a child to move on is one of the main tasks for foster carers but it can often be painful. If carers are helped to acknowledge their feelings and to manage them, they can in turn help the child do the same.

There can be a tendency to talk to children about all the good things that moving to a permanent placement will bring, and to avoid any painful, ambivalent feelings a child might have. It will be more helpful if children are allowed to express and discuss negative feelings as well as positive ones, to avoid them receiving the message that negative feelings are not valid or acceptable. If foster carers say that they will miss the child and be sad when they go, but also glad that they will have a family of their own, it will give the child permission to have similar feelings and to express them.

Timing

Older children will usually benefit from longer introductions – it can take weeks or even months to get to know each other. At the beginning, the prospective parents should visit children in the foster home. Only when the children feel confident enough should they visit the parents in their home-to-be before staying overnight and for weekends.

The timing of moves for children who are in school requires careful thought. Holiday periods may seem best for the child but may be the times when social workers and other professionals have arranged to take leave, and the child and family could find themselves without full support during this critical time. It will sometimes have to be an "on balance" decision but, in general, children manage better if they can adjust to their new home before they also have to cope with a new school. On the other hand, long school holidays without structured activities can be overwhelming for new families.

It is vital to tailor introductions to the needs and personality of each individual child and to avoid the pressure of adult agendas to do with work schedules, foster carers' holiday plans, change of social workers or bureaucratic convenience.

activities

17

Timetables

Children can find visual material particularly helpful in the run-up to a move. Use 24-hour clock exercises to enable them to have a realistic understanding of timetables and what is going to happen next.

Make a "moving calendar" with the child – use a sheet of A4 paper for each week and divide it into days. Use words or drawings to depict what will be happening on that day, for example, place a drawing or sticker of a car on the day of the child's first planned visit to the new family's home. A cup of tea can illustrate the day the adopters will come to spend the afternoon.

Older children can keep a diary or lists of "things to do". They can be given photographs (and can take photographs themselves during visits) of the prospective family and home and put them into the diary or a "moving scrapbook".

Questions

Children will not think of all their questions at the same time. Help them by giving them a "What I want to know" activity sheet or exercise book which they can decorate or colour. They can write down (or get their carers to note down) their questions as they think of them. Questions might include:

- Can I take my bike/toy pram/PlayStation/rabbit?
- Will I have my own bedroom?
- Can I watch TV before I get dressed on Saturday mornings?
- Who will pick me up from school?
- Who will know that I am being adopted?
- What will I say at my new school?
- Can I still see my grandma?

Information about living with the child and daily routines should be given by the foster carers to the new parents in the child's presence. This will be particularly important if the child is concerned about a specific matter and needs to know what a new family might think about it and how they will react.

CASE EXAMPLE
JOHN

John used to smear his faeces on the wall. He was also enuretic. He was afraid that if his new carers knew they would not want to look after him. He hadn't done it for over a year but it was the reason for a previous placement breakdown. His foster carer asked his new family, in front of John, how they felt about that. John was reassured to hear his new carers say that they could understand why this might happen to a little boy, it was something they could manage and would not stop them from caring for him.

If the introductions have been positive, the aim will be to help the child gradually to let go of the familiar old world and begin to invest in the new family. This will include saying goodbye to many significant people such as teachers, friends and neighbours. Whilst this is an important part of the process, it is prudent to be aware of the possible impact of repeated farewells on children who may already be anxious about leaving. Foster carers will often hold a special event like a tea party. If the prospective parents can be invited, it will give people who know the child the opportunity to show their approval and to wish the new family well for the future.

Again, all the child's possessions – even those which are battered, torn and tattered – should be carefully packed for the move. If the child does not own a suitcase or backpack they should be able to choose their own luggage for the move. Children should never have to put their possessions into black plastic bags.

Preparing children for a return home

Foster carers can sometimes lose heart when they perceive that a child is returning to a poorer family environment. It can be hard to remember that the plan to return children home has been assessed as the best way to meet their welfare needs. The move will be jeopardised if the child is put in the position of having to compare their home with the foster home. It is always important not to be inappropriately critical of the child's birth family and circumstances, particularly when they are preparing for a return home.

If some of the issues that originally precipitated the child's move from home are still unresolved, the child will need strategies for dealing with them. It is helpful to explore with the child the things that will probably go all right and other things that may be more difficult. For instance, a member of the family may have left or perhaps a new baby has arrived: big changes such as these may make for additional worries or, alternatively, can ease the situation considerably.

Carers need encouragement to know that their efforts and the progress made by children will not have been wasted. Children cherish their memories of positive times with adults. A temporary nurturing relationship can give children who have learned not to trust the confidence to move on. Many of us remember a teacher who made a real difference to our lives, notwithstanding that it was a temporary relationship.

We know that children are able to develop and maintain a number of relationships if there is positive regard between the adults involved. But sometimes what can seem to be a most natural aspect of relating to other people can pose big difficulties for children.

CASE EXAMPLE
NOEL

Noel asked his foster carer if he could "practise" looking at his new parents. He knew he was shy and not very good at looking at adults when speaking to them. His foster carer had been working hard with him to overcome this. His prospective parents joined in with the exercise. Noel started by looking at them only when he wanted permission to do something or if he was unsure what to do next. His new parents explained that they were also practising looking at Noel and enjoying it. This demonstrated that it was possible to get things right. In time, looking at each other became a natural thing to do.

activities

Jigsaw/cards prompt games

Various manufacturers produce cards/jigsaw games about family life and moves between homes. You can use these play materials as a basis for preparing children for both practical and emotional aspects of the forthcoming move. As with the other games and activities, the session can be repeated to reinforce messages and to allow children to deal progressively with new thoughts and concerns.

Contact with carers post-placement

The question of whether it is in the child's interests (and whether the child wants) to remain in touch with foster carers after a move should be addressed as part of the transition plan. It is rarely advisable to sever meaningful connections and to add to the list of a child's losses. Whatever arrangement is agreed, it will be important to review it periodically as the child grows up and needs change.

Children at the stage of "magical thinking" (see Chapter 4) may try to make sense of unexplained moves by believing that their foster carers have died or did not really love them. New parents should reinforce the message that the carers are well, that they miss the children but that they are also very happy because the children now have their own family.

Name changes

It is important that children are consulted about possible name changes and how and when this might happen. Our names often have special meanings for us and changing a child's name when many other significant aspects of their life are also changing can add unnecessarily to their sense of loss, anxiety or confusion.

Adopted children generally, but not necessarily, take on the surname of their new parents but legally this cannot take effect until the adoption order is made. Sometimes the child becomes 'known as…' but no documentary changes should be made before the order. Social workers and adoptive parents should talk with older children and young people about a name change and discuss whether they wish to keep a former surname, either on its own or in combination with the new family's name.

Changing first names is generally discouraged. If there is a good reason why a child's first name should be changed, the name should be kept as an additional middle name. The fact that new adoptive parents find it difficult to pronounce a child's given name is not sufficient reason to change it.

Disengaging

Social workers

Relationships with social workers and other professionals can be of real importance to children. When a social worker withdraws, children may be anxious about losing the anchor the worker provided during turbulent periods.

Jewett (1994) reminds us:

> 'If you help a child who is not your own…you will probably become a trusted friend and source of support…you must be sensitive to the child's vulnerability when terminating the relationship. Like any loss, separation from the helper should be expected and gradual. It should not leave the child…feeling helpless but should be planned with the child's participation.'

Ending the work with a child should not come as a surprise. Children should be clear throughout about the nature of the social worker's role, and that their involvement is time-limited.

However, when the time comes to draw to a close a piece of direct work with the child, it can still be difficult. A child or young person may be sad, miss their worker, or be uncertain about coping without them.

When you disengage from a child you should:

- remind the child well in advance that you will be reducing the frequency of visits and will be making a final visit shortly;

- give time and space for the child to express how they feel about the forthcoming separation from you, even if they can't wait to be rid of all social workers;

- talk about the adults who will be continuing with the work and support of the child.

If a child is moving to an adoptive family, it is good practice and in line with adoption guidance to write a letter (a later life letter) for the child to read when he or she is older and may want to know more about the circumstances of their adoption. The letter should be given to the adopters and a copy placed on the adoption file.

18

Later life letters

Later life letters should include:

- An introduction: This should cover the social worker's role and your involvement with the family.

- A clear summary of the child's background: This should describe simply any attempts that were made to reunite the child with his or her birth family, explain why the child could not continue to be cared for by their birth parents, set out what subsequently happened to parents and siblings, and list any contact the child had with various family members before and after placement.

- The legal situation: This should give details of the legal status of the child before and after adoption. It is important to note the dates of final hearings. Who was present and what did they say? When was the adoption order made and what did the judge do?

- Family finding: Children like to know how their family was found and how important it was to find the right family.

- Conclusion: The letter can finish with an invitation for the child to make contact for more information and with very best wishes for the child and their new family. The letter should be signed by the social worker.

CASE EXAMPLE
THOMAS

Office address

Dear Thomas,

You probably won't remember me, but my name is in your life journey book, and I knew you when you were a baby. This letter will tell you about what happened to you before you came to live with your mum and dad.

Your birth mother, Michelle, met your birth father, Huw, during an evening out while her partner, Pete, was serving a prison sentence for theft. The relationship between them was a very short one, and Michelle did not tell Huw that she had become pregnant.

You were born on Monday 24 March 2003 at 2.30 in the afternoon at the Queen Elizabeth Hospital in Newport. It was a glorious spring day, but there had been a thunderstorm the night before your birth. Michelle had still not told anybody about her pregnancy and felt unable to look after you. She wanted you to have love, security and a happy life, which she did not feel able to give. She made the very difficult decision that it would be better for you to be cared for by a mother and father who would be able to give you a better chance in life. Michelle named you Thomas because that was her surname.

I met you when you were two days old. You were a happy, contented baby with fair hair, blue eyes and a dimple in your chin, like your birth mother. Michelle looked after you for the four days you were in the hospital with her and she fed you from a bottle. You left the hospital on Friday 28 March, and went to stay for two days with Lilian, who was a foster carer. Your birth mother gave you a teddy and kissed your cheek. After two days with Lilian you went to stay with Mary and Richard, who were also foster carers. They were very fond of you; you were a baby who gurgled and slept a lot.

When you were with Richard and Mary, Michelle visited you – she thought that you looked like her! She also thought you looked like your half-sister, Whitney, who is a year older than you and lives with Michelle. After the visit, Michelle began to ask herself if she had made the right decision. She had a photograph taken of you and her together that she kept in her purse.

Michelle had lots of friends and enjoyed drinking coffee and talking. She was, however, very frightened of Pete, her partner, and thought that if she took you home you would be a constant reminder to him that she had looked for comfort and been close to someone else while he had been in prison. After a lot of thought and discussion, she decided that she would not able to protect and care for you properly.

I saw you every week while you were living with Mary and Richard. You smiled at six weeks and loved the "twinkle twinkle" mobile your birth mother had given Mary and Richard to put over your cot to help you get to sleep. I took the picture of you being fed by Mary – the one with baby rice all over your face – that is in your life journey book.

A lot of information was put together about you and Michelle and this was given to a judge in court. He had to consider it carefully, which took a long time, because there were such important decisions to be made. Finally, the judge said that it would be better for you to live with a new family and to be adopted. Michelle was sad, but felt that this was the best thing for you and she was happy knowing that you would be loved and looked after. She was also glad that your mobile would go with you to be placed over your new cot.

I found out about Will and Jane and Abigail and went to meet them. I thought that Will and Jane would be good, loving parents for you – and Abigail really wanted a little brother. You met Will and Jane when they came to see you at Richard and Mary's home, and I remember you sleeping in Will's arms. You were all smiling.

I last saw you in August 2004 in your new home when you were 18 months old. You were happy, contented and smiling. I enjoyed the time I spent with you; you were always glad to see me and every time I hear "twinkle, twinkle", I think of you!

I hope that this helps you to understand a bit more about how you came to live with Will, Jane and Abigail. They have lots more information about Michelle and your birth family and will be able to answer your questions. The adoption team at.......can be contacted by telephone on........or by email at.......and would always be pleased to hear from you.

With very best wishes for your future.

Yours sincerely,

Name

Social Worker

Foster carers

Disengaging from a child who is returning home

Whether the child has been looked after for a short time or a longer time will affect how they experience the move back home. Unless children have not been willing or able to establish a relationship with foster carers, they will find it difficult to leave.

One of the ways we cope with the hurt of separations is to start distancing ourselves before we actually leave. This is called anticipatory grieving. Not only the child, but the foster carers and other children in the home may be apprehensive about the imminent parting.

Anticipatory grieving includes being sad or anxious (about self and others) and creating a wider emotional distance; you may find that there are more family squabbles prior to the child's move. Children will need to be reassured that they will be able to cope and that you will help them to make it a positive move (see Chapter 17 for further details).

Talk about the move and how to manage partings with the whole family. Reassure all children about the plan. No matter what difficulties there may have been in the placement, make sure you all have proper "goodbyes" and that the child is able to take away any pictures, letters, photographs and other mementos of their time with you.

If there is to be future contact, make the initial arrangements before the child leaves; if not, the child should go with your best and warmest wishes, even when the placement ending comes as something of a relief.

Helping children move to an adoptive placement

Foster carers are extremely important members of the team of people involved in preparing a child for a move to an adoptive placement (see Chapter 17). You may have mixed feelings about the forthcoming move, especially if you have cared for children since infancy and they regard you as a parent. Some social workers and others may not appreciate the degree of emotional involvement between foster carers and children when it has always been clear that the child will be moving to an adoptive placement. You can experience many varied emotions – happiness, worry, doubts, anger, delight, hope and, in some cases, heartache. Try to make sure that, as well as your supervising social worker, you have family and friends who can support you.

Many children who are adopted unfortunately do not have ongoing direct contact with previous foster carers. But this need not be the case. Children should never sustain an unnecessary loss; they need to know that they will not entirely lose old relationships before committing themselves wholeheartedly to new ones. Arrangements for contact with carers should be part of the introduction plan, and foster carers need both training and support to work sensitively with adoptive parents following the move.

Making sense of disruptions

'Placements are like marriages, there are no guarantees of success.'

(Fitzgerald, 1983, p 6)

Disruption is the term used to describe a foster placement or adoptive placement that has ended in an unplanned way; Whilst disruption is invariably a time for intense feelings of regret, anger, guilt, shame and failure, it is also important to regard it as part of the process of family placement from which lessons can be learnt in order to enable the workers to plan more effectively to meet the child's needs.

Around 20 per cent of all adoptions disrupt. The rate rises to almost 40 per cent for children who are aged 9–11 at the time of placement. Disruptions can happen during introductions or at any time following placement either before or after an adoption order is made, and can happen for a number of different reasons.

If children are removed from a placement quickly, with little or no explanation or understanding of why things have not worked out, it will revive their earlier fears of moves that they did not understand. If a child does not have an explanation of why things have happened, they may feel it must be their fault. If the prospective family is left feeling they are to blame, they will not be able to support the child. If social workers are not supported by their managers, they will be wary of taking risks in the future. Effective disruption meetings and structured support are essential for all parties to feel heard and respected and enabled to learn and move on from disruption.

Look at the case study in Chapter 5 which tells Mark's story.

- Which elements could have contributed to the placement disrupting?

- What input might have helped the placement to survive?

- What lessons could be learnt from Mark's story?

- How would you explain this to Mark?

Whe the foster carer was working with Mark to draw his ecomap, it was necessary to encourage Mark to include all the significant people in his life. He only wanted to put down the carers he had lived with before he moved to the adopters. He didn't want to include either his birth family or the adopters and clearly felt rejected by almost everyone.

It was important to help Mark talk about his pain. His play was very destructive and instead of using the play wand for wishes he wanted to attack and pretend to kill people with it.

Mark also regressed in his behaviour and often curled up in a foetal ball behind the sofa.

He would only talk to the hand puppet he'd been given for Christmas and this became his way of communicating for several weeks after the disruption. Mark also grieved for his sister, Kelly, and said that he wanted to live with her.

Abrupt moves from one home to another should be regarded as the exception rather than the rule.

Indications for a planned disruption are:

- the adoptive family is not able to meet the child's needs after receiving all available help and counselling;

- the adoptive family insists on the child's removal and does not want to deal with the problems.

CASE EXAMPLE
REBECCA AND JOHN

Rebecca and John were eight and ten years old when their adoptive parents felt unable to continue caring for them. The placement had lasted for 18 months. It was important that the adoptive parents told the children that they could no longer care for them. The children were not surprised because they knew things were not going well. The social worker used the feeling cards faces and asked the children and carers how they felt. They all pointed to "sad" and John and the adults pointed to "guilty". Rebecca pointed to "scared". They were all able to talk about their feelings and take responsibility for their part in the relationship, and consider how they could manage their sadness and the parting and remember each other.

It is important to establish how a child has experienced being parented by the adopters.

- What did the child need?

- How was the adoptive family trying to meet those needs?

- What was working well?

- Were things working well for everybody?

- What was not working for the child?

If at all possible and suitable, a return to the previous foster home should always be considered as first choice after a disruption. In some cases, unresolved grieving for the foster carers may have caused the problems in the adoptive placement, and a return to the foster home is just what the child wanted. A clear assessment of the child's needs after disruption should inform planning for the child's future.

Disruption happens. It is rarely attributable to a single cause or event and most permanent placements do not disrupt.

> Claire, a confused four-year-old whose placement ended after six months, pretended it never happened; her prospective adopters said she had lived like a stranger in their midst. After the disruption, Claire never spoke of the family she had just left; she was compliant in her new foster home and the foster carer described her as a 'very independent, intelligent and capable little girl who is a joy to look after'.

The danger is that young, appealing children like Claire may be placed quickly again in an attempt to avoid drift in care. But Claire needed an intensive and lengthy spell of play therapy before she was ready to trust herself to be parented. She had never dealt with the separation from her birth family, her traumatic memories, and could not deal with this most recent disruption (taken from Argent and Coleman, 2006). However much practice improves and resources increase, disruption will never be eradicated – personal relationships, by their very nature, can never be predicted.

What we can do is help children to make sense of the experiences that they have undergone, using direct work and therapeutic techniques, to better prepare them for the future.

References

Argent H and Coleman J (2006) *Dealing with Disruption*, London: BAAF

Brodzinsky M and Schechter Marshal D (eds) (1993) *The Psychology of Adoption*, Oxford: Oxford University Press

Cairns K (2002) *Attachment, Trauma and Resilience*, London: BAAF

Comfort Randy Lee and staff at Our Place: a centre for families who foster and adopt (2004) *Playing to Learn – Learning to Play*
For availability contact Ourplace1@btconnect.com

Department of Health, Department for Education and Employment and Home Office (2000) *Framework for the Assessment of Children in Need and their Families*, London: The Stationery Office

Department of Health, Department for Education and Employment and National Assembly for Wales (1999) *Working Together to Safeguard Children: A guide for inter-agency working to safeguard and promote the welfare of children*, London: The Stationery Office

Fitzgerald J (1983) *Understanding Disruption*, London: BAAF

Gilligan R (2001) *Promoting Resilience*, London: BAAF

Jewett C (1994) *Helping Children Cope with Separation and Loss*, Harvard: Harvard Common Press

Kahn H (2002) *Tia's Wishes*, London: BAAF

Kahn H (2003) *Tyler's Wishes*, London: BAAF

Kanter Joel (ed) (2004) *Face to Face with Children: The life of Clare Winnicott*, London: Karnac Books

Kosonen M (1996) 'Maintaining sibling relationships: neglected dimension in child care practice', *British Journal of Social Work*, 26, pp 809–822

Laming H (2003) *The Victoria Climbié Enquiry: Report of an enquiry by Lord Laming*, Norwich: The Stationery Office

Morrison M (2004) *Talking about Adoption to your Adopted Child: A guide for adoptive parents*, London: BAAF

National Assembly for Wales (2005) *Practice Guidance on Assessing the Support Needs of Adoptive Families*, Cardiff: National Assembly for Wales

Neilson Jacqueline (1973) *Older Children need Love too*, London: Association of British Adoption Agencies

Neimeyer R A (2001) 'Meaning reconstruction and loss', in *Meaning Construction and the Experience of Loss*, Neimeyer RA (ed) Washington DC: American Psychological Association, pp 1–12

Ryan T and Walker R (2003) *Life Story Work: A practical guide to helping children understand their past*, London: BAAF

Thomas C and Beckford V with Lowe N and Murch M (1999) *Adopted Children Speaking*, London: BAAF

Welsh Assembly Government (2004) *Safeguarding Children: Working together for positive outcomes*, Cardiff: Welsh Assembly Government

Bibliography

For use with children and young people

Argent H and Lane M (2003) *What Happens in Court?*, London: BAAF

Argent H (2004) *What is Contact?*, London: BAAF

Argent H (2004) *What is a Disability?*, London: BAAF

Byrne S and Chambers L (1997) *Living with a New Family: Nadia and Rashid's story*, London: BAAF

Foxon J (2003) *Nutmeg gets a Letter*, London: BAAF

Kahn H (2002) *Tia's Wishes*, London: BAAF

Kahn H (2003) *Tyler's Wishes*, London: BAAF

Lidster A (2995) *Chester and Daisy Move On*, London: BAAF

Sambrooks P and Orritt B (2000) *Dennis Duckling*, London: The Children's Society

Shah S (2003) *Adoption: What it is and what it means*, London: BAAF

Life story work

Betts B and Ahmed A (2003) *My Life Story*, CD-ROM, Orkney: Information Plus Ltd

Camis J (2001) *My Life and Me*, London: BAAF

Information Plus Ltd (1998) *Bruce's Multimedia Story* CD-ROM, Orkney: Information Plus Ltd

Shah S and Argent A (2006) *Life Story Work: What it is and what it means*, London: BAAF

Disruption

Byrne S and Chambers L (1997) *Hoping for the Best: Jack's story*, London: BAAF

Guides for adults to use

Education

Cairns K and Stanway C (2004) *Learn the Child: Helping looked after children to learn*, London: BAAF

Life story work

Ryan T and Walker R (2007) *Life Story Work*, London: BAAF

For adopters

Morrison M (2004) *Talking about Adoption to your Adopted Child*, London: BAAF

Thomas C and Beckford V with Lowe N and Murch M (1999) *Adopted Children Speaking*, London: BAAF

For social workers or foster carers

Argent H and Coleman J (2006) *Dealing with Disruption*, London: BAAF

Cairns K (2002) *Attachment, Trauma and Resilience*, London: BAAF

Fahlberg V (1994) *A Child's Journey Through Placement*, London: BAAF

Gilligan R (2001, forthcoming 2007) *Promoting Resilience*, London: BAAF

Jewett C (1995) *Helping Children Cope with Separation and Loss*, London: BAAF/Batsford

Lord J and Borthwick S (2001) *Together or Apart? Assessing brothers and sisters for permanent placement*, London: BAAF

Neil E and Howe D (2004) *Contact in Adoption and Permanent Foster Care*, London: BAAF

Appendix 1

Communication tools and age groups

Children who are pre-verbal or who have limited vocabulary

Sand/water play

Glove/finger puppets

Play-people/dolls

"Shoebox" houses

Road/path play mat and cars

"Feelings" faces/masks

Mirror

Photographs/magazine pictures

Children aged 4–10 (primary school age)

Any of above, plus:

Memory box

Clay/play-dough modelling

Toy telephones/walkie-talkies

Life graph, pathway, footprints, birthday cakes

Ecomap

Life journey book

Art activities – drawing, painting, collage

Board/card games

"Likes"/"Dislikes" lists/games

Joint story-telling

Genogram

Writing a contract

Children aged 10+

Any of the above, plus:

Keeping a diary

Role play/miming

"One-to-ten" scales of feelings/emotions

Fill in sheets/questionnaires

"Advantages"/"Disadvantages" lists

Different adults' parenting roles

Appendix 2

Index of activities

Index of activities	PAGE
"This is us" album	19
Genogram	22
Feelings faces	43
Keyleigh's "sweet swaps"	46
Life journey work – life graphs and pathways	46–50, 91
Memory boxes	54
Understanding others	54
This is me	65
The child's story	65
Joint story-telling	68
Expressing feelings	68, 86
Questionnaires	69
A "Now" calendar/timetables	73, 98
Photographs and life journey books	76
My best holiday	77
Piles of love	77
Workbooks	78
"Don't like/Like" lists	80
Ideas for maintaining indirect contact	80
Feelings pictures	86
A family tree	88
Circles	91
Life pathways	91
Gemma and Sophie's ecomap	93
Jigsaw/cards prompt games	100
Later life letters	102

Appendix 3

Suggested contents for workers' "tool kits"

Ideally, each childcare team and foster home should have a box containing the essential tools for undertaking preparation work with children. The following is a list of items that could be in such a box. Some of these items can be used generally with a number of children; others should remain the property of the child and will therefore need to be renewed.

Agencies need to identify money in their budgets to finance the purchase of a tool kit box. The total cost of the items listed below is approximately £100.

Foldable road play mat

Doll families – a mixture of ethnicities

Finger or glove puppets

Toy telephones

Small cars

Paints, brushes, scissors

Play-dough/clay

Wand

Felt-tip pens/crayons

Old magazines

Plastic/cardboard box (large enough to hold mementos, etc)

Album for photographs/drawings

Sheets of plain and coloured paper

A diary

Stickers

Suitable boxes to make houses (e.g. shoeboxes)